A DEFINING MOMENT
Transnational Nursing Education

Dr Nirmala ARUNASALAM

For Western universities TNHE can be seen as a cash cow; for receiving countries it can be a cost-effective way of quickly raising the level and status of home produced professionals. But, for the recipients, in this instance Malaysian nurses upgrading from diplo-ma to degree level qualifications, it can be an inter-cultural nightmare, one which the flying faculty charged with its delivery are not necessarily equipped to deal with. The author's personal and professional experience of straddling and then crossing those boundaries informs this exploration of Malaysian nurses' perspectives on their TNHE experiences, and the implications that these have for the learning and teaching provided. **– Mary Thornton, Professor Emeritus, University of Hertfordshire, UK**

This book is an insightful exploration of an example of transnational higher education which identified some key questions that need to be asked about such programmes. As both an insider and outsider in relation to the culture and the profession the researcher is able to uncover a range of participant experiences and perceptions which highlight the importance of intercultural awareness on the part of flying faculty. Paying close attention to curriculum and pedagogy in terms of assumptions, expectations and prior experience is shown to be essential. The complexity of teaching and learning in transnational contexts and the challenges involved in attempting to use such programmes to bring about practice change are clearly identified. **– Joy Jarvis, Professor of Educational Practice, University of Hertfordshire, UK**

This book raises important issues regarding the possible mismatches between the agenda of transnational higher education institutions who are selling their courses across the world. The main attraction of some of these courses tends to be the high status of a western degree, as opposed to the relevance and usability of the course materials in highly contextual local practice settings.

One of the interesting aspects of this research is the unique consideration of the role of researchers who are able to blend an insider's understanding with an outsider's overview on the situation concerning Malaysian nurses. The theory practice divide is at the crux of this research. The voice of Malaysian nurses and their experiences of TNHE modules is used to expose the mismatch between the experience, needs and contextual understanding between the nurses in their practice situations and the theoretical positions taught by 'flying faculty' western academics. The difficulties the students subsequently have in putting theory into practice is an interesting aspect of this research.

The book demonstrates some of the dangers which are evident in the all too eager embrace by western TNHE providers to offer partnerships in the delivery of higher education. Such advances are equally eagerly embraced by governments eager to heighten the status of their nation by importing western degrees, at times with-out consideration of specific local needs. **– Dr Bushra Connors, School of Education, University of Hertfordshire, UK**

A revealing and important book for anyone interested in transnational higher education. At the heart of this book is an in-depth qualitative study of Malaysian nurses' views and experiences of TNHE. The book will be of crucial interest to educators, policy makers, researchers and students involved in transnational education. – **Dr Oscar Odena, Reader in Education, University of Glasgow, UK**

Arunasalam delivers a competent and accessible text focusing on nurse education. Within one of the toughest professions to work in, the author provides the spaces for Malaysian nurses to reflect upon classroom training and practical experiences. This is also an exploration and critique of internationalisation and quality control regarding nurse training courses within and between the UK, Australia and Malaysia. Recommended for teaching and learning as well as pedagogical courses at undergraduate and postgraduate levels. – **Dr Richard Race, Roehampton University, UK**

I became familiar with Dr Arunasalam as an examiner of the Doctoral thesis produced which informs this text. The nature of trans-national education is a topic that she demonstrates much passion about. The Malaysian context is discussed and dealt with sensitively in relation to the topic, and her cultural, nursing and educational backgrounds contribute to this. The approach taken shows application of qualitative research approaches in data collection, analysis and conclusions derived, making a contribution to the literature in transnational education. – **Associate Professor Robert Burton, Griffith University, Singapore**.

I am familiar with Dr. Arunasalam's work, having had the privilege of working with her on a collaborative qualitative research study. The depth of the background for this study, and the intimate self-reflection Dr. Arunasalam provides for this monograph greatly enhances the quality of the study. As a Malaysian, United Kingdom resident, nurse, academic, and practitioner-research, she brought a wealth of understanding and insight into this study as she continued to learn from her interviewees. Her revealing of the influence culture and context have on nurses' preference to learning, and the time it takes to adjust and adapt to new ways of teaching and learning is clearly explicated. Dr. Arunasalam has a keen interest in the theory-practice connection, and this is evident in her research. Her use of qualitative research as a mode for understanding this phenomenon is clearly appropriate. She is an expert in this field of research and has a grasp for its use unlike any nurse researcher I know.

Important issues emerged in this study that can have an impact on the continued growth of health care in Malaysia and the delivery of nursing education through TNHE. There is a clear gap in assumptions and expectations between the Malaysian students and the TNHE educators. This monograph is a significant contribution to the dearth in the literature about the TNHE post-registration programs, and to the gaps in literature addressing the voice of those involved in this partnership. It is a high quality piece of research that is a significant contribution to the body of knowledge related to nursing education. – **Thayer McGahee, Dean, School of Nursing, University of South Carolina Aiken.**

Nirmala Arunasalam's book is a testimony of a highly qualified nurse with migrant background for nurses' claim to self-determination in education all over the world. The reader dives into the living world of Malaysian nurses and their perceptions of a Higher Education program. As a German nurse I felt deeply touched by Nirmala's close description of Malaysian nurses' perceptions of a state-financed educational program with the goal to get access to the high standard of nursing education in countries with top-level nursing educational programs and strong political representation of nurses. There are economic, societal, political and even cultural requirements for nurses' education. But only the nurses themselves are allowed and are able to formulate the goals, the outcomes and the contents of their own education, both academic and occupational.

Nirmala Arunasalam's book is a mile stone in education research with the focus on equal education opportunities and transcultural aspects. Nursing as a worldwide vital profession for sustainable, national healthcare systems and its development as a highly qualified profession is the aim of the programmes evaluated.

It is a must have and a must read in a world of "pseudo factum knowledge" where social and human oriented professions and scientific disciplines such as nursing are getting little attention. It is not only a solid research report but a final speech for self-determination of nurses seeking for transnational accepted higher education degrees.

It is a book not only for nurses but for all of us who feel responsible for the societal challenge to handle socio-demographic changes, worldwide migration flows, globalization and health related external influences such as climate change, high workload, and social disparities. To allow nurses to get an internationally accepted occupational and academic degree is not only a question of equal educational opportunities but a question of the sustainable development of health care systems all over the world. – **Astrid Herold-Majumdar, Professor, Munich University of Applied Sciences, Germany**

The book's focus is Transnational Higher Education teaching, learning, theory and practice experiences of the nursing workforce in Malaysia. It shows a new model for post-registration education in Malaysia to improve the education, status and professionalism of the nursing workforce in parity with other healthcare professionals. This book will inspire all individuals who have a commitment to teaching and learning as it is both informative and enjoyable. The author's knowledge and experience on the subject is very impressive. At the same time the deep and trusting experience of the writer on the subject deeply affects us. – **Dr Elif Iskender, Associate Professor, Istanbul Beykent University, Turkey**

A DEFINING MOMENT
Transnational Nursing Education

Dr Nirmala ARUNASALAM

TRANSNATIONAL PRESS LONDON
2017

A DEFINING MOMENT: Transnational Nursing Education

By Dr Nirmala ARUNASALAM

Copyright © 2017 by Transnational Press London

All rights reserved. This book or any portion thereof may not be reproduced or used in any manner whatsoever without the express written permission of the publisher except for the use of brief quotations in a book review or scholarly journal.

First Published in 2017 by TRANSNATIONAL PRESS LONDON in the United Kingdom, 12 Ridgeway Gardens, London, N6 5XR, UK.

www.tplondon.com

 Transnational Press London® and the logo and its affiliated brands are registered trademarks.

This book or any portion thereof may not be reproduced or used in any manner whatsoever without the express written permission of the publisher except for the use of brief quotations in a book review or scholarly journal.

Requests for permission to reproduce material from this work should be sent to: sales@tplondon.com

Paperback [US Edition]

ISBN: 978-1-910781-63-0

Cover Design: Gizem Çakır

www.tplondon.com

Contents

Acknowledgements	ii
About the Author	iii
Introduction	1
Chapter 1. Setting the scene	3
Chapter 2. Exploring the background	11
Chapter 3. Revealing my roles and stances	53
Chapter 4. Unfolding Malaysian nurses' views	75
Chapter 5. A Defining moment	115
Conclusion	125
References	127
Index	147

Acknowledgements

I give my heavenly Father all praise, honour and glory. Lord Jesus, I thank you as only through you have I been able to write this book. To you gentle Holy Spirit, I thank you for every word written.

Grateful thanks to Professor Ibrahim Sirkeci for the opportunity to write this monograph based on my doctoral thesis, "A Defining Moment: Malaysian Nurses' Perspectives of Transnational Higher Education". A word of thanks to family, friends and colleagues for your support in helping me to write in a reader-friendly way.

I am grateful to the following publishers for permitting extracts from the published journal articles to be reprinted in this book:

Arunasalam, N.D., (2017). Malaysian nurses' views: Local versus Transnational Higher Education. Border Crossing. 7(1). 188-205.

Arunasalam, N.D., (2017). Reflexivity: Personal, professional and researcher stances. SAGE Research Methods Case Health. SAGE Publications Ltd. London.

Arunasalam, N.D., (2016). Technology enhanced learning in Transnational Higher Education Programmes. British Journal of Nursing. 25(21). 2-6.

Arunasalam, N.D., (2016). Shhh …… silence …… is normal in Transnational Higher Education classrooms. LINK journal. 2(2). 1-3.

Arunasalam, N.D., (2016). Malaysian Nurses Evaluation: Trans-national Higher Education Programmes. British Journal of Nursing. 25(6). 337-340.

Arunasalam, N.D., (2016). Malaysian Nurses Motivation to Study on Transnational Higher Education Programmes. Malaysian Journal of Nursing. 7(2). 34-41.

Arunasalam, N.D., (2015). Impact of UK and Australian Trans-national Higher Education in Malaysia. Journal of Studies in International Education. 1-18.

Dedication

A Defining Moment: Transnational Nursing Education is dedicated to my late dad (who would have been so proud), my mum Saraswathy, my family and friends: thank you for your love, support, motivation and for recognising God's mercy and grace in my life.

About the Author

Dr Nirmala Devi Arunasalam a Senior Lecturer in Nursing based at the University of Plymouth. She was a visiting research fellow at Regent's University London Centre for Transnational Studies in 2017. Mala has 13 years' experience teaching in a range of undergraduate and postgraduate nursing programmes as a Senior Lecturer in UK Higher Education. Dr Arunasalam serves on the editorial board of *Border Crossing* journal. Dr Arunasalam is a member of the Organizing Committee for The Migration Conference series (www.migrationcenter.org). Mala's keenness to develop networks has led to developing an international exchange programme, collaborative research and/or publications with University of South Carolina Aiken, USA, University of Applied Sciences Munich, Germany, Regent's University London, Griffith University, Singapore and Malaysian nurses who had studied on local, UK and Australian Transnational Higher Education degree programmes.

Introduction

To improve the education, professionalism and status of nursing internationally, nurse education is shifting away from the diploma qualification to become a graduate profession. The change will better prepare nurses to meet the complex and diverse needs, care environments, technological tools and information management systems of patients and ageing populations. Nurses also collaborate and coordinate patient care with teams of healthcare professionals, so their qualifications need to be in parity with those professionals. Post-registration top-up nursing degree programmes enable trained nurses who had previously attained their diploma qualifications to upgrade to a degree level. Such bridging programmes are provided both full-time and part-time but most nurses opt to study part-time as it allows them to develop professionally whilst continuing to work.

In the current globalisation climate of competition to raise international profile and income-generating contracts, it has become a trend for western Nurse Education universities to identify education needs in the Asian region and develop collaborative links. One such collaborative connection has been with certain UK and Australian Nurse Education universities to provide part-time post-registration top-up nursing degree programmes in Malaysia. It is due to the limited local part-time provision of these programmes. The Malaysian Ministry of Higher Education and the Malaysian Nursing Board embraced these programmes to enhance their graduate level nursing workforce. Further, a western degree is desirable because of the prestigious reputation of western nurse education.

Outline of this book

In Chapter 1, I outline the impact of globalisation on higher education. A summary is provided of pre-registration programmes in the UK, Australia and Malaysia and the TNHE post-registration top-up nursing degree programmes delivered in Malaysia. My reasons for studying this topic, the research aim and question is given. At the heart of this book is the collaborating Malaysian nurses' views of their experiences in the classroom, theory-practice connection and evaluation of TNHE programmes. In this book, the word 'western' is only used to signify Britain (UK) and Australia.

Chapter 2 will explore, discuss and critique the internationalisation agendas of the UK, Australia and Malaysia (focusing on TNHE) and standards of quality control. It is followed by the relationships between nurse education and training programmes within and between the three countries. Finally, the cultural influences on TNHE teaching and learning and the provision of care are addressed.

Chapters 3 to 6 are presented in this way to provide insight and transparency of my influence on the research and the research process. Chapter 3, reveals how my personal, professional and researcher stance authorise me to speak. It provides knowledge, rationale and meaning to the nurses' unique voices in Chapter 4. Further, it gives clarity to descriptions and ensures the claims I make in Chapter 5's conclusion is valid.

Chapter 1. Setting the scene

Global, international, and transnational are often used interchangeably with different aspects of cross border affairs. Similar confusion exists in Higher Education (HE). Sirkeci (2013) defines transnationalism from a perspective of connectedness through space in a dialectic way: "the links between the global and the local in a world of nodes denoting the transnational space" (Sirkeci, 2013:3). Transnational space is a connected place where needs and wants are addressed through optimal use of benefits and resources arising from the connectedness in a virtually borderless world of actors (Sirkeci, 2013:vii). Hence, this is the space where transnational higher education takes place while benefiting from global integration and yet addressing the local and/or national needs and wants.

The impact and response to globalisation has led to the internationalisation of HE, "... the process of integrating an international, intercultural or global dimension into the purpose, functions or delivery of post-secondary education" (Knight, 2003: 21). In the context of HE, internationalisation involves diverse types and methods of education delivery.

To reflect internationalisation, some United Kingdom and Australian Nurse Education universities have attempted to capitalise on the prestige of their nurse education, pioneering professional practice and development, and HE for working adults (lifelong learning). Their aim, according to Hogan (2012), is to increase their influence, profile, market expansion and income generating contracts through collaborative links with Malaysia. Some of these initiatives are to deliver TNHE post-registration nursing top-up degree programmes. The United Nations Educational, Scientific and Cultural Organisations (UNESCO's) / Council of Europe's (2002: 2) Code of Good Practice in the Provision of Transnational Education define TNHE as *"all types of higher education study programmes or set of courses of study, or educational services ... in which the learners are located in a country different from the one where the awarding institution is based"*.

In recent years, Malaysian government policy called for the upgrading of nursing qualification and improving the quality of health care services (Harrar, 2016). To support this, the Malaysian Ministry of Health (MMoH) offers a monthly graduate allowance of RM$400 as an incentive to qualified nurses to upgrade their Diplomas to Degree level. In tandem with this policy call, in 2008, Continuous Professional Education as a criterion for nurses' annual re-license was enforced by the Malaysian Nursing Board (MNB).

However, it was recognised that there were a) a lack of part-time courses to upgrade hospital-based diploma trained nurses to degree level (Coomarasamy, Wint and Sukumaran, 2015; Yaakup, Eng, and Shah, 2014) and b) insufficient professional development opportunities (Chong, Francis, Cooper and Abdullah, 2014; Chong, 2013).

The MNB, private Higher Education Institutions (HEIs) and private hospitals embrace TNHE post-registration top-up nursing degree programmes from developed western countries. This is to enhance the education, professionalism and status of the profession to meet the National Vision Policy (Vision 2020). In brief, Vision 2020 was an idea adopted by a previous Prime Minister, Tun Dr Mahathir Mohamed in 1990. It illustrates Malaysia's commitment to achieve a developed country status by changing the mind-set of nurses through a graduate level nursing workforce (Mohamed, 1991). There is also the potential for nurses to obtain a high status western degree with reduced costs (Gill, 2009; MNB, 2008). Malaysia also expects the TNHE programmes to provide western expertise and innovation as a benchmark against international standards (Malaysian Nurses

Association, 2010; Ismail, 2006). It is expected to improve provision of patient care and to minimise the risks for patients and nurses.

Rationale for study

This study was initially motivated by a request from a UK university for expressions of interest to teach in TNHE post-registration top-up nursing degree programmes to be delivered in Malaysia. I identified two 'flying faculty' academics, selected to deliver teaching within one to two weeks for one module, to be part of a small-scale study that I undertook at that time (Arunasalam, 2009). The research explored academics' knowledge and understanding of the influence cultural values can have on nurses' preferences to learning.

The research findings showed that the academics made assumptions, for example that nurses on TNHE programmes would possess the language and subject knowledge to understand immediately the taught theory. Neither of the academics considered how the short one or two-week teaching period might affect the nurses. This is because evidence shows students struggle to concentrate for long periods of time (Biggs, 2014; Bligh, 2000).

The academics also did not recognise the differences between western and Malaysian teaching and learning methods (Nieto, 2010). The western teaching and learning approach is learner-centred. Critical thinking, analysis and reflective practice is vital to this approach that is also supported by evidence in the form of resources such as research based journals. Western assessments require nurses to discover information from a variety of sources, to debate and justify arguments using academic writing practices (Montgomery, 2016; Hyland, Trahar, Anderson and Dickens, 2008). In contrast, the Malaysian nurses were used to a teacher-centred approach that focused on learning by memorising to demonstrate the knowledge gained from the teacher and textbook (Sundler, Pettersson and Berglund, 2015; Varutharaju and Ratnavadivel, 2014) in order to pass examinations. The nurses were expected easily to switch from their totally different teaching and learning mode and connect with a new western educational way (c.f. Healey, 2015).

The UK, Australian and Malaysian nurses, in both clinical and educational settings, have agreed for years that taught knowledge must be related and relevant to clinical settings (Karstadt, 2011; Birks, Chapman and Francis, 2009a; Egan and Jaye, 2009; Flanagan, 2009; Croxon and Maginnis, 2007). Some studies have even acknowledged that theoretical knowledge is directly related to the ability to perform in the clinical context (Brown, 2014; Cotterill-Walker, 2012; Mantzoukas and Jasper, 2008; Banning, 2008). This highlights the importance for the nursing theory taught in the classroom to be understood and applicable to practice settings (Schober, 2013; Leininger, 2011; Birks, Chapman, Francis, 2009b) to ensure safe and quality nursing care. The two academics seemed to believe that the TNHE taught theory based on the western values of nursing and in line with their professional bodies was relevant and adequate within the Malaysian setting.

Standards in nursing practice worldwide are governed by the World Health Organisation (WHO). In reality, the fundamental key points of care are not shared worldwide, rather they are determined by individual countries' core values and beliefs (Birks, Chapman and Francis, 2009b; Chiu, 2005, 2006; Birks, 2005). Theoretical knowledge and professional standards in the UK and Australia prepare nurses to function within the nursing culture of the UK and Australia (Gijbels, O'Connell, Dalton-O'Connor, and O'Donovan, 2010). In contrast, Malaysian nurses are expected to integrate their clinical practice in line with the WHO's and MNB's (2002) professional standards and the traditions of their diverse ethnic groups (Hishamshah, Rashid, Mustaffa, Haroon and Badaruddin, 2011; Chee and Barraclough, 2007). The TNHE theoretical knowledge based on UK and Australian post-registration Nurse Education standards (Nursing and Midwifery Council, 2011; Nursing and Midwifery Board of Australia, 2016) are not similar to Malaysia.

This realisation led to my unravelling and rewinding specific childhood and adult memories and personal and professional experiences from both Malaysia and the UK. It led to my identifying similarities and differences through experience to raise consciousness (Walker, 2010; Birks, Chapman and Francis, 2009a).

Thus, the research focus was changed, from an institutional perspective to the Malaysian nurses' views, a strand that appeared to be *"hidden from public view"* (Seale, 2004:72).

Aim of the study

This research aimed to explore Malaysian nurses' views of the extent to which TNHE theoretical knowledge taught in post-registration top-up degree programmes, is applied in clinical settings. To make this possible, it was essential to identify nurses' experiences in the TNHE teaching and learning environment and the theory-practice connection in the care of multicultural, multiracial and multilingual patients (Teras, 2013; Srinivasan, 2012; Abdullah and Koh, 2009). It was analysed within the context of my own experiences as a Malaysian, student nurse, UK resident, trained nurse, nurse academic and practitioner-researcher working in a UK HEI.

Initially, four UK universities were identified to be part of the research in Malaysia, but gaining consent proved to be a complex and lengthy process with largely negative responses. Eventually, only one university provided written agreement to participate in my study. Whilst I was collecting data in Malaysia, interest was shown by some nurses who had studied with other TNHE universities, one UK and one Australian. These nurses had completed their programme of study within six months of data collection. They were accepted into the study, and were also asked to suggest further participants or to introduce others who had been in similar programmes, as they were not accessible to me through other sampling strategies.

Research question

The research question was to identify to what extent Malaysian nurses have applied theoretical knowledge taught in TNHE post-registration top-up nursing degree programmes in clinical settings. To answer the research question, four key areas of the nurses' views were considered to be important and meaningful. These were: personal development; professional transformation; implementation; and acceptance of nurse-led changes. Personal development and professional transformation were considered main motivators for these nurses to pursue further study as it improves their personal image and professional socialisation (Chiu, 2005; Birks, 2005).

Acceptance of nurse-led changes was included due to a previous UK study by Hardwick and Jordan (2002), and an Australian study by Glass (1998) that revealed how hostility and tension with colleagues who did not have degrees impeded the application of learnt knowledge in practice settings. Further, Sturdy and Gabriel (2000) argue that Malaysians resist western practices due to former colonial status and Juhary's (2007) belief of the keenness to maintain a unifying national identity. In addition to the four pre-determined key aspects, during analysis of the data other relevant and interesting themes in relation to the research aim also emerged.

Pre-registration nurse education

In the past, nursing knowledge was acquired through apprenticeship type training where nursing and clinical skills were taught and learnt during clinical placement or work on a hospital ward. The move to HE for nursing was supported by the International Council of Nurses (ICN). The ICN stress, "*university preparation is essential if nursing is to receive the public trust as a profession and, accordingly, be granted the accountability and rewards of professionals*" (ICN, 2008: 12). Each school of nursing initiates and develops their own undergraduate programmes for student nurses that reflect their preferred approaches to curriculum development and implementation. Thus, they vary between providers/ universities within and between countries.

However, all pre-registration nursing programmes have an integration of theoretical and practical knowledge. The theoretical knowledge is acquired in academic settings to enable understanding of what is being done and why (Brown, 2014; Cotterill-Walker, 2012). On the other hand, practical or process knowledge is learnt in clinical settings (Schober, 2013). In nursing, both the theoretical and practical knowledge are developed in parallel to enable application of the knowledge in an integrated and meaningful way in patient care. This means the theory must be context-based to allow the nurses to process knowledge in their nursing practices (Leininger, 2011; Birks, Chapman, Francis, 2009a).

In Malaysia, student nurses in diploma and degree pre-registration nursing programmes are required to complete a three year diploma programme, or three or four year degree programmes of study. On completion of their studies, all nurses in either diploma or degree programmes are required to take the national Lembaga Jururawat Malaysia [translated as Malaysian Nursing Board examination. Passing this examination [assessed at Diploma level only] allows diploma and degree nurses to register with the Malaysian Nursing Board. They are given an annual practicing certificate at diploma level and are known as Registered Nurses or Junior Nurses.

By comparison, both diploma and degree student nurses in the UK are required to fulfil theoretical, clinical and professional criteria as laid down by their professional body, the Nursing and Midwifery Council (NMC) (2010). It is interpreted by each individual HEI providing pre-registration nurse education. In order to register with the NMC and attain the title Registered Nurse, a nurse's specialisation, rather than their academic level (diploma or degree) is recorded. This is similar in Australia. But, in Australia their diploma pre-registration nurse education programme was quickly replaced, after two years of implementation, by degree pre-registration programmes. Student nurses are only assessed by their HEIs and attain the title Registered Nurse on registration with the state nursing board, which has now been replaced by the Australian Health Professionals Regulation Agency (AHPRA). AHPRA oversees the national Australian Nursing and Midwifery Council (ANMC).

TNHE post-registration top-up degree programmes

The worldwide trends for trained nurses is focused on a move from diploma to a degree level of training and continuing professional education to ensure a well-educated nursing workforce. Dugdall and Watson (2009) stress that the development of evidence based critical reasoning, and advanced knowledge and clinical skills improve the professional status of nurses and meet the demands and complexities of modern healthcare. At national and professional level, diploma registered nurses affected by the pre-registration education change are given the option to meet the new standards through post-registration top-up nursing degrees. These top-up degrees are bridging programmes that allow trained nurses to upgrade their diploma qualifications (240 credits) to a degree level (360 credits) through successful completion of a number of modules or credits, usually 15 or 30, allocated to each module. The nurses' registration to practice does not change.

Previous research (Helms, 2008; Dunn and Wallace, 2008) suggests that UK and Australian TNHE providers are likely to take modules 'off the shelf' from existing programmes that mirror their curriculum and assessments. Customisation is only made to meet the necessary regulatory frameworks of host countries as their concern is to maintain quality standards, academic norms and assessment strategies, etc, similar to home students. Ohmori (2004) stresses that the concern is to ensure integrity and identical value of the awards. Based on an insight from one UK university school of nursing participating in this study, the modules selected for the different top-up degree awards are part of existing programmes in the UK. Some adaptation has been made to the Module Syllabus in an attempt to meet the MNB and Malaysian Qualifications Agency (MQA) requirements. Malaysian nurses who complete the 100% theory programme attain an academic award; however, it does not warrant registration to practice in the UK by the UK Nursing and Midwifery Council or in Australia by the Australian Nursing and Midwifery Council because it lacks clinical assessment.

Chapter 2. Exploring the background

The internationalisation agenda

World-wide socio-economic factors have led to reduced government funding per student, vast growth in student numbers and the blurring of the university-polytechnic divide (Leask and Carroll, 2011; OECD, 2010). They have also changed the focus of many HEIs, including in the UK and Australia, towards economic and political market expansion, global recognition and the raising of international profiles. Not surprisingly, and as argued in supporting literature, this has narrowed the construct of HE internationalisation as it has undermined the integration of global, international and intercultural dimensions (Knight and Morshidi, 2011; Marginson, 2011). In this latter understanding of what internationalisation should mean for HE, 'global' refers to cross-cultural graduates with the skills to work in a diverse world; 'international' pertains to TNHE programmes, distance learning, mobility of academics and students with an international component in programme content; and 'intercultural' refers to outlook and issues of a diverse society (c.f. Knight, 2004).

Offshore programmes enhance social justice by providing opportunity to students in developing countries to access a qualification not otherwise available to them. However, many like Bone (2008) believe the shift of focus of internationalisation by some western HEIs, has led to attempts to capitalise their reputation, prestige of nurse education, pioneering professional practice and development, and HE for working adults (lifelong learning). Mainly, their aim is to increase their profile, market expansion and income generating contracts through collaborative links (Garrett, 2015; Caruana and Montgomery, 2015; Lasanowski, 2009; Knight, 2008). It has resulted in short-term mass recruitment of students at the risk of neglecting core areas of teaching, research and learning, and the tarnishing of academic reputations of some UK and Australian HEIs (Altbach and Knight, 2006).

The tension between these two understandings of what HE internationalisation can or should be is pertinent to Malaysia. Aligned precariously with it is the Malaysian government's focus on national transformation and re-structuring of its own HE system (Arif, Ilyas and Hameed, 2013) while controlling public expenditure. In 2009, Gill reported that Datuk Seri Najib Tun Razak, then Deputy and currently Prime Minister of Malaysia, believed the presence of foreign campuses such as those from the UK and Australia would expand the private HE sector and inspire it to improve its own potential, strength and calibre of students. This is because the Malaysian government and society consider qualifications from an English-speaking country to be prestigious: a way of advancement for a knowledge-based society and providing benchmarking for international standards (Mok and Yu, 2013). An influx of foreign programmes increases their HEIs' ability to attract the target number of 100,000 international students to develop an international HE hub. These aspirations align themselves with the broader definition of HE internationalisation and demonstrate the acceptance of TNHE programmes operated by and located in Malaysia.

Questions raised were whether TNHE programmes integrate the global, international and intercultural dimensions of the internationalisation agenda. In addition, whether these aspects were considered when approving TNHE programmes.

Transnational Higher Education (TNHE) and quality control

'TNHE', 'offshore', 'cross-border', 'trans-border' and 'borderless' have been used to describe the real or virtual movement of providers, institutions, academics, students, curricula, projects, programmes, knowledge, materials and values (cultural, institutional, educational, procedural and perceptual) from one country to another (Knight, 2004). The term 'TNHE', first used by the Global Alliance for Transnational Education in 1999, is the term most widely accepted and used within policy frameworks and regulations across both national and regional jurisdiction borders. In reality, TNHE is often misunderstood with no common understanding, definition or approach. It appears to have many relationships with different sorts of providers, rationales, outlooks, strategies, programmes, mechanisms, delivery and awards. All are components of an international education system, simply with a different emphasis in response to globalisation.

TNHE has a close relationship with the Bologna Declaration, its follow-up process and intended goals. A joint guideline by UNESCO and the Organisation for Economic Co-operation and Development (OECD) outlines that the programmes provided must consider both access and relevance to the national context (Ziguras and Mc Burnie, 2015; OECD, 2010). However, no legal framework is available for TNHE collaborative partnerships, their educational structures, quality and standards of programmes or qualifications awarded. In Malaysia, policies related to the nation's development framework led the government, in the late 1990's, to put strategies in place for the regulation of TNHE provisions, often offered (but not always) in association with overseas awarding bodies (Morshidi, 2006).

Malaysia appears to assume TNHE provision brings with it prestige, international quality standards and expertise to re-invent itself by shaping its HE to promote national development goals (Mok, 2008; MQA, 2009). The difficulty, as the literature above suggests, is that western internationalisation prioritises economic and market expansion while raising international profiles which Bone (2009) believes may override the need or ability to provide excellence in exported teaching and learning. Bone's concern appears to have some foundation as in practice there are negative accounts of TNHE programmes, with criticisms that it is purely for commercial exchange. It is because TNHE universities market their existing degrees with limited consideration towards the four fundamental gaps that Knight (2004) states need to be bridged i.e. language, culture, geography and history. Only superficial changes are made to internationalise the curricula, with limited local references to social, cultural and traditional practices (Ziguras and Mc Burnie, 2015; Wang, 2010). The values, beliefs, teaching styles and assessments are suitable to the western context which Knight (2011) argues as being disrespectful to the students and a blatant commercialisation of an existing programme.

The emphasis should be on balance between integrating social, cultural and educational needs to ensure that what is taught has relevance to the students and the same quality assurance as western educational programmes (Mok and Yu, 2013). The aims of TNHE programmes should be to broaden students' frames of reference, facilitate them to internalise the practices of the new culture of learning, and to mediate between and mobilise the two learning cultural resources. This in effect means to create new forms of learning to enable them to embrace these practices within their prior learning. This has brought its own set of difficulties.

Many UK and Australian universities began their TNHE collaborations with distance education programmes designed for their local students (Ziguras, 2007). It appears that only limited consideration had been given to the UNESCO and OECD (2005:14) *Guidelines for Quality Provision in Cross-Border Higher Education* that state awarding institutions should:

> *"Ensure that the programmes they deliver across borders and in their home country are of comparable quality and that they take into account the cultural and linguistic sensitivities of the receiving country. It is desirable that a commitment to this effect should be made public."*

This refrain, that TNHE provision is mainly a commercial exchange rather than an integration of international social, cultural and educational endeavour, questions their appropriateness. Also questionable is their quality, applicability and effectiveness to meet the human resource needs of Malaysia's national economy, as outlined in Vision 2020, the national plans and the industrial master plans. Further, as acquiring cultural values is tacit, and even problematic because it involves intellectual humility and cognitive endeavour, TNHE providers prefer to reflect their HEI's internationalisation strategies (Hill, Cheong, Leong and Fernandez-Chung, 2014).

There is a general belief that TNHE programmes are protected by national regulations and standards and codes of practice. Thus, the importance for the curricula of TNHE programmes to be similar to those delivered in the home country or suitable revisions made to suit the student group and the local context (Bennett et al, 2010). This notion appears straightforward. In reality, there are challenges to conforming to different regulatory frameworks of collaborating countries. This is because it is difficult to ascertain the degree of similarity or difference between programmes due to the educational, language and cultural variations where the TNHE programmes are delivered. In short, there is no one-size-fits-all model of quality assurance. This may be contributing to evidence that some TNHE providers avoid aspects of the national accreditation restrictions of the countries receiving these programmes (Leask and Carroll, 2011; Marginson, 2011; Mok, 2008; Knight, 2008; Leask, 2005, 2003). It has led to the potential mismatch between programme contents and the host country's social norms and regulations (Smith, 2009). This in turn neither enhances the global, international and intercultural student experience nor reveals that the programmes are credible or that their credentials are internationally recognised. What has become apparent is that TNHE providers' opportunistic programme developments are income generating in the short-term but may not be sustainable long-term as their quality assurance systems are *ad hoc* and reactive in manner.

UK, Australian and Malaysian pre and post-registration nurse education

Professional nursing bodies in UK, Australia and Malaysia (NMC, ANMC, MNB), shape the pre-registration nurse education, standards and registration and post registration professional development requirements, annual re-licensure and regulatory mechanisms. The similarities and differences in the pre and post registration nursing programmes in the three countries involved in my research will be identified and discussed.

UK pre-registration nurse training and education

In the pre-1990s' UK, three year nurse training programmes were the responsibility of schools of nursing associated with hospitals. Theoretical knowledge was taught in parallel with nursing skills that were learnt through hands-on experience in general, psychiatric, child and learning disability practice settings. On qualifying, in addition to registration, hospital-based schools of nursing provided nurses with a certificate from the United Kingdom Central Council (UKCC) (1986). Often, registered nurses sought to obtain certificates also in other specialities.

The transfer of nurse education from the traditional schools of nursing into HE settings in the UK began in 1989, in line with other countries such as Australia. It ensured UK nurses would not be left behind (UKCC, 2001). Around the same time, polytechnics were amalgamating with or becoming fully-fledged universities, e.g. The London Polytechnic became the University of Westminster. Universities offered student nurses three year diploma or degree programmes, or four year degree nursing programmes, in their chosen branch of specialty i.e. Adult, Child, Mental Health or Learning Disabilities. The move into university education meant that the apprenticeship style of nurse training was abandoned in favour of students having a university-based education. Students were no longer regarded as part of the hospital workforce in practice settings (UKCC, 2001). The curricula differed between HEIs, but the content covered met the registration requirements of the then professional body, the UKCC, and, after 2002, the NMC. There was no national examination and student nurses were assessed by their individual HEIs. On completion, they attained an academic award from their university and registration as a Registered Nurse in their field speciality with the previous UKCC (1986), and in 2002 the NMC.

Initially, a three year university-based diploma programme became the chosen route to registration as a nurse. This is because, financially, the non-means-tested bursary and maintenance grant was more lucrative than the means-tested bursary and student loan available to students on degree programmes. In addition, degree programmes had a higher entry criteria and assessment level. This changed in 2008 when the NMC stipulated that all new nurses qualifying in England from 2013 must have the minimum award of a degree. Both diploma and degree nurses take on similar roles as trained nurses.

Australian pre-registration nurse training and education

Until the 1980s, Australian nurses were trained for three years in hospital nursing schools and were paid employees of the parent hospital (Dooley, 1990). On completion, a certificate was awarded in addition to registration in their specific field (Australian Nursing Council (ANC), 1994). Many registered nurses went on to hold general, psychiatric, midwifery or other certificates, known as a double (DC) or triple (TC) certificate to signify this attainment.

The transfer of nurse education to HEIs occurred at varying rates in each state and territory with diplomas for entry level nurse education. In late 1980s, only a select few Australian HEIs started offering three-year undergraduate degree programmes leading to registration as a Registered Nurse (RN) throughout Australia and RN Division 1 (Div.1) in Victoria, to practice in general, medical, surgical, psychiatric and developmental disability nursing (Lynette, 1990).

The rapid introduction of pre-registration degree programmes (after two years) led to diploma nurses being given the option to upgrade their qualification to a degree level. There was no national licensing examination. Each state had a statutory authority that accredited individual university programmes against the requirements of that authority. These statutory authorities and nurses' registration boards were supported by state governments but operated independently through state legislation (Stein-Parbury, 2000).

In 1992, to regulate nursing standards and processes nationally, the ANC represented by each of the eight state and territory nurse regulatory authorities was established. All registered nurses working in Australia are required to demonstrate the ANMC's national competency standards. The standards provide a framework for assessing competency and are used to assess a nurse's eligibility for annual renewal of their licence to practice and for involvement in professional conduct matters. Mainly, these standards are used by HEIs to develop curricula to assess student and new graduate nurses' performance (Australian Qualifications Framework, 2002). The Australian Nursing and Midwifery Accreditation Council (ANMAC), previously known as Australian Nursing and Midwifery Council (ANMC), is now the sole accreditation authority for the nursing and midwifery professions under the National Registration and Accreditation Scheme (NRAS). The Nursing and Midwifery Board of Australia regulates professional registration, codes, standards, and competency (ANMAC, 2012).

Malaysian pre-registration nurse training

In Malaysia, the nurse education originally was modelled on that of the UK, and has developed along similar lines and continues to be influenced by the trends and literature from the UK. However, it has evolved to suit the traditional and cultural rules of the country, of which only certain elements remain to maintain the standards the government expects. In line with other developed countries, to improve the quality of nursing practice in the provision of patient care, the traditional certificate awarded on completion of a basic three year hospital-based training was replaced with diploma courses in the early 1990s (Shamsudin, 2006).

Despite the transfer of traditional apprenticeship hospital-based nurse training to diploma courses, these courses have remained as hospital-based nurse training. Four year degree level pre-registration nursing courses are available only at selected universities. The cost, limited number of places on these degree courses, and labour force requirements mean the majority of student nurses from public and private colleges of nursing still enter the profession and qualify for entry to registration, at diploma level. On completion of their pre-registration diploma courses, nurses are encouraged to undertake six months' or one year's post-basic education to gain in-depth knowledge and clinical experience in specialised areas. Further, it allows them to consolidate their training in a clinical environment.

To enable nurses with diplomas to upgrade their qualifications, Malaysian public universities provide full-time top-up degrees, with only one university providing a part-time option. The full-time programmes are funded by the government with the nurses then either entering a contract or being bonded to the government for double the time taken to complete the degree. The part-time programme is self-funded because employers are reluctant to sponsor a local part-time programme. Both the local full-time and part-time programmes have a clinical practice component and Honours title incorporated in their programmes.

In comparing the nurse training and education programmes offered in the UK, Australia and Malaysia, there are a few distinct differences and similarities. In the UK, there is no national examination for student nurses; instead they must pass both their theoretical and practice learning outcomes as set by their individual HEIs. These HEIs send transcripts of their results to the NMC for student nurses to be registered. In the UK, all nurses register under a given part of the NMC Register relevant to their original field (e.g. Part 1 - Adult, Part 2 – Child, Part 3 – Mental Health and Part 4 – Learning Disability) whether they were on diploma or degree programmes (NMC, 2004).

Similarly, in Australia where the diploma pre-registration nurse education programme was replaced by degree programmes, there is no national licensing examination. Instead the statutory authority in each state accredited individual university programmes against the specific requirements of that authority, and the title Division 1 Registered Nurse was attained on registration (Australian Nursing and Midwifery Board, 1981; ANC, 1994). Registration with the individual state nursing boards has been replaced by registration via AHPRA which oversees the national Australian Nursing and Midwifery Board and other Health Care Professions. Once a student has successfully met the course requirements and is eligible for registration, they will be required to lodge an application for registration. In October 2012, the Nursing and Midwifery Board urged student nurses about to graduate as nurses to go online four to six weeks before completing their programme of study to enable a smooth transition from study to work. In comparison, student nurses in both diploma and degree pre-registration training programmes in Malaysia are required to take the national Lembaga Jururawat Malaysia, or Malaysian Nursing Board, 100 multiple choice questions examination. It is assessed at diploma level on completion of their three or four year programme of study.

The view in the three countries was that nurses with diplomas were not expected to meet the new degree standard, but they did have the option to top up or upgrade their qualifications. There was also no financial incentive or automatic salary increase for nurses in the UK and Australia, but it became apparent that the degree increased one's chances of promotion (Mc Hugh and Lake, 2010). When academic qualifications increased, some nurses were motivated to study as part of their personal and professional development in order to fulfil their moral and legal responsibility to update their knowledge, skills and status, and for professional survival (Pullen, 2011). As national requirements in Australia and the UK became a degree-level entry, there was potential for diploma nurses to lose out in the job or promotion market due to competition. In Malaysia, it has become a bureaucratic target to meet the human resource needs of the national economy, as outlined in Vision 2020 (MNB, 2008; Jantan, Chan, Shanon and Sibly, 2005). Recognising that only two percent of the nursing workforce had degrees, the Ministry of Health offered a financial incentive of a graduate allowance of RM$400 per month to encourage a rise of between 10 to 15 percent of diploma nurses trained to degree level.

In all three countries, these top-up degrees often were delivered in the evening either by block course, or once a week, or at weekends. It was either face-to-face teaching or distance learning or a mixture of face-to-face and distance mode according to the registered nurses' personal and employment constraints. Nurses were funded or financially supported by their practice settings for the duration of the degree course through their salaries and time release, whilst self-funding nurses were allowed some flexibility for working patterns.

Post-registration nursing requirements

Professional development is the process of promoting leadership to enhance the advancement of the nursing profession (Schober, 2013). Nursing professional bodies worldwide stipulate continuous professional development to maintain credentials, standards and competencies and to avoid obsolete practices in the delivery of patient care. The term and requirements for professional development differ for each country, as evidenced below.

UK post-registration Continuous Professional Development

The UK, NMC, expects all nurses to assume responsibility throughout their professional lives for their continuing professional development. Nurses are required to undertake a minimum of 35 hours of post registration education and practice (PREP) every three years for annual registration. PREP utilises a critical model for continuous theoretical learning that enables nurses to constantly modify their knowledge base to relate to and support their practice in practice settings and the changing health care environment (NMC, 2011). Opportunities to gain additional clinical skills after qualification are also available. The national standards, HEIs and NMC collaboratively identify ways of fostering partnerships that ensure the education of nurses draws from and feeds into standards of proficiency for safe and effective practice.

Australian post-registration Continuing Nursing Education

The ANMC works with the state and territorial nursing regulation authorities to govern the practice of nursing and to facilitate a national approach. Recently, the Royal College of Nursing Australia, in an attempt to upgrade qualifications, enhance lifelong learning and specialisation in the area of clinical interest, has extended its Continuing Nursing Education (CNE) program to all in the nursing profession. The state and territory Nursing and Midwifery Regulatory Authorities require all registered nurses working in Australia to demonstrate the Australian Nursing and Midwifery Accreditation Council's (2010) 20 hours of self-directed, or institutional, or active learning per year in order to renew annually their licence to practice. No restrictions are stipulated on the type of CNE activities. But, nurses must demonstrate review of their practice, meet required learning needs and ensure the relevance of the activity and its likelihood to enhance their area of practice.

Malaysian post-registration Continuous Professional Education

In 1998, the MNB stipulated in the Nurses' Code of Conduct, the voluntary requirement of 10 contact hours in CPE activities annually, but many nurses did not voluntarily update their professional knowledge (Chiarella, 2002). In 2008, the MNB implemented guidelines and legislation for mandatory Malaysian Continuous Professional Education (MCPE) in an attempt to improve skills, education and implementation of evidence based practice in line with globalisation. Nurses must complete 35 hours of CPE annually to renew their license of practice, based on a Credit Points System where different activities are awarded varying points.

In all three countries, nursing practice is defined and governed by law, and entrance to the profession is regulated at the national or state level by professional bodies. However, they vary as elements of knowing are socially/culturally and physically situated. Thus, the recommendation of Race (2011; 2013), Burton and Kirshbaum (2012) and Burton (2009) that cultural diversity should be recognised and used to shape education policy is pertinent. Despite the differences between the pre-nurse educational programmes within the three countries in my research, it is clear that all involve the study of nursing theory and clinical skills for application of learning in practice. Professional development requirements for nurses in these countries may vary, but all emphasise the need for continuous advancement of their knowledge base and skills to support their clinical practice and for annual registration.

TNHE post-registration nursing degree programmes

Increasing emphasis on education and significant changes in healthcare worldwide led to qualification escalation to ensure that equal respect was accorded to nurses as to other health professionals (NMC, 2011; ANMAC, 2010; ICN, 2008; MNB, 2008). The MNB, private colleges linked to private hospitals, private HEIs and public universities collaborate with UK and Australian HEIs to accept these top-up programmes. Both the UK and Australia market the post-registration top-up degree programmes separately, as their method of delivery is different from those provided for degree student nurses (NMC, 2011; ANMAC, 2010). The varied specifics of HEIs in the UK and Australia, with their different curricula and mode of delivery, appeared not to affect where these diploma nurses chose to study; but, the TNHE university chosen was either selected by their employer or was their preference if self-funding.

TNHE top-up degree programmes in Malaysia

TNHE post-registration top-up degrees are bridging programmes that do not change nurses' registration to practice as a nurse (NMC, 2011; ANMAC, 2010; MNB, 2008). These programmes allow the Diploma or level two of 240 credits to be increased to a level three with 360 credits required for a degree. It is achieved through a number of modules or credits, usually 15 or 30, allocated to each module. Thus, supporting the continuous development and lifelong learning that professional nursing bodies stipulate to maintain registration for quality patient care.

Some private hospitals promote TNHE post-registration nursing degree programmes as part of their in-service training or as four stand-alone modules, because a nursing degree has become the basic required qualification (MNB, 2008). These in-service programmes do not require Malaysian Quality Agency (MQA) approval. MQA approval is only sought when these programmes are marketed as a Degree programme (MQA, 2009). In relation to my study, some participants were in programmes provided by their employers that did not require MQA approval. Others, who funded their own study, participated in programmes with a TNHE university that had accreditation approvals. These nurses used their savings or took out loans to fund their TNHE studies. In contrast, nurses in government hospitals that provide post-registration degree programmes in public universities, are fully government sponsored and tend to study full-time, unless they choose to study part-time. Private hospital nurses also have the option to study full-time in public universities, but have to self-fund. Most opt to study part-time (all of my interviewees) because they choose, or their employer provides the TNHE programme. It reflects the actual difference of Malaysian Continuous Professional Education for post-registration top-up degrees between government and private hospitals.

To undertake the TNHE pathway or any stand-alone modules, nurses must have prior registration with the MNB, a Diploma in Nursing or the ability to provide alternative evidence (MoHE, 2007-2010). The Module Syllabus provides information about learning outcomes and a guide to the core knowledge and professional values essential and implicit to the module and assessment. It is to provide students with knowledge and understanding. Nurses in top-up degree programmes were only required to complete the theoretical components that include research, management and professional contents related to advancing practice and sometimes specific to a clinical specialty. Essentially, it is similar to undergraduate programmes. There was no need to undertake any practicum but nurses are required to relate their western assessments to their western clinical settings. (NMC, 2011; ANMAC, 2010).

In Malaysia, where these programmes are provided mainly full-time with limited part-time provision, all nurses have theoretical knowledge taught in the classroom and experiential learning in practice settings (MNB, 2008; MoHE, 2010). In addition, they undertake and complete a research project for the Honours title. Both Birks (2006) and Chiu (2005, 2006) stress that, with a limitation to flexible off-campus or part-time study, many health care employers and nurses have opted for TNHE programmes for the diploma to degree conversion. The MQA (2009) and MNB (2007) attempt to indigenise the international curricula in line with its national objectives when the programmes are offered nationally. But, this is not seen when it is provided as a professional development programme for nurses by their employers.

In the final chapter, evaluating the TNHE post-registration top-up degree programmes, these issues will be re-considered. They are important for the Malaysian Ministry of Health, Ministry of Higher Education and the Nursing Board because their investment in TNHE programmes is aimed at attaining a graduate workforce to enable knowledgeable nurses with changed mind-sets to enhance standards of patient care, the incentive behind increased demands for these professional development courses in the UK, Australia and Malaysia.

Questions raised were whether UK and Australian TNHE programmes had integrated global, international and intercultural dimensions into their TNHE taught theory. It is also essential to explore the extent to which TNHE theory improved the knowledge of Malaysian nurses who had engaged in them and, by association, patient care.

Motivation to undertake top-up degree programmes

Studies in the UK, Australia and Malaysia of nursing students studying in post-registration top-up degree programmes have been considered from a multifaceted and inter-related range of perspectives (Birks, 2006; Chiu, 2005; Delaney and Piscopo, 2004). Consistent with UK findings, Boore's (1996) study revealed that 80% of nurses were motivated by the theory-practice relationship and the potential to improve their competence. 20% were inspired by the opportunity for promotion. In contrast, Dowswell, Hewison and Hinds (1998) study indicated that nurses, midwives and health visitors felt personal (intrinsic) motivation, including the desire for academic stimulation and life-long learning. Professional (extrinsic) motivation involved career progression and the need to support junior colleagues and student nurses.

Another UK study by Hardwick and Jordan (2002) showed nurses were driven by their professional development needs of research, using computers and inter-disciplinary team-working. Supporting Australian studies, Chaboyer and Retsas (1996) evaluated a critical care course. Nurses believed the course increased their opportunity for promotion.

Pelletier et al's (1998) Australian study indicated motivating factors were: job satisfaction or personal (42%); increased professional status (22%); and promotion (17%). A survey of 101 practising nurses in Australia (Delaney and Piscopo, 2004) showed personal and professional growth as reasons to obtain a degree. A raised level of professionalism was identified but was outweighed by improved knowledge and self-image based on achievement and success.

In contrast, in Malaysia, a study by Chiu (2006), a Malaysian living in Australia, used semi-structured interviews and focus groups from an Australian TNHE post-registration nursing degree programme. This programme included a practice component that enabled nurses to spend four weeks in an Australian clinical setting. It revealed nurses' aspirations were for personal and professional growth and a short residential block experience at the host university campus. The degree was recognised as key to gain knowledge and achieve professional advancement, improve practice and gain higher qualifications and professional status. Mainly, the professional development arising from international experience was reported to contribute to a deeper insight of nursing issues, as the Australian-taught theory was directly relevant to the international experience.

Another study by Birks (2005), solely with westerners, used semi-structured interviews of a UK TNHE post-registration nursing degree programme. The programme had only a theoretical component. It showed nurses were motivated to enhance their knowledge, improve personally and professionally and implement learning in practice. A recent study by Chong, Sellick, Francis and Abdullah, (2011) with both local and westerners being part of the research team, reviewed the motive for nurses to attend local post-registration degree programmes. Their quantitative self-explanatory structured questionnaire showed nurses' motives were to give quality care to patient, update their knowledge and to achieve professional status.

There were differences between the three studies. As an insider and outsider to Malaysia, Chiu (2006) found the interview and focus group data identified that nurses' aspirations were mainly for personal and professional growth. In contrast, Birks' (2005) outsider influenced interview findings showed implementation of learning in practice was the nurses' motivation for undertaking the programme. The findings showed no indication of resistance to western practice ways in clinical settings. On the other hand, the quantitative self-explanatory structured questionnaire used by Chong, Sellick, Francis and Abdullah, (2011) of a local programme with a practice component showed that nurses' motives were to give quality care to patients and to improve their skills in practice.

Theory-practice connection

Schwab (2004: 107) defined theory as a structure of information that is linked with models, meta-theory, principles, concepts and methods which should enable students to learn about work, for work, and through work to justify their actions and to ensure that what they are doing is in context. Louis Pasteur said in 1854, *"without theory, practice is but routine born of habit"*. The standards derived from the World Health Organisation enable nurses to carry out their role, assess patient needs, plan interventions, apply theories and principles within the boundaries of their practice and to evaluate outcomes of patient care.

Workplace knowledge, in the situated perspective, thus exists socially and "is not something that we can claim as individuals . . . this competence is experienced and manifested by members through their own engagement in practice" (Wenger, 1998: 137). Wenger's belief adds a key point to Schwab's definition; that the knowing from theory must engage with social communities, as an individual's knowledge, thoughts, actions and insight are influenced by their culture and the national context. Wenger's (1998) view is supported by Kramsch (2017). Kramsch highlights the importance of recognising this as individuals have difficulty relinquishing previously constructed cultural perceptions, beliefs and behaviours when attempting to adapt to a new culture: in this case TNHE, a proposed community of practice. Wenger and Kramsch raise the question that is pertinent to my research: Does the TNHE taught theory include aspects relevant, related and acceptable to the Malaysian perspective, practice and provision of patient care in clinical settings. This is further expounded by Biggs (2014), that to achieve functioning knowledge (for professional activities in practice settings), it is vital to have declarative (relevant knowledge base), procedural (skills necessary to apply) and conditional knowledge (awareness to relate to appropriate circumstances).

Nursing, being a practice-based profession, requires both theoretical and practical knowledge. Theoretical knowledge is the knowledge that all nurses acquire to understand what they are doing and why, whilst practical knowledge is learnt in the clinical area. Both theoretical and practical knowledge must be developed alongside each other to enable application of the knowledge in an integrated and meaningful way in patient care. Karstadt (2011) describes the theoretical knowledge presented in academic settings as 'viable knowledge'. Phillips, Schostak and Tyler (2000) describe the practical knowledge observed in clinical practice as 'process knowledge'. There has always been an implicit assumption by nurses in educational and practice settings that a certain degree of theoretical knowledge is required (Gribben, McLellan, McGirr and Chenery-Morris, 2017; Reed, 2012; Karstadt, 2011; Dyess and Chase, 2010; Birks, Chapman and Francis, 2009a; Egan and Jaye, 2009; Flanagan, 2009; Croxon and Maginnis, 2007). This is supported by Eraut (2004). Chiu (2006) agrees, and stresses that integration of theoretical and practical knowledge is a pre-requisite in clinical situations as it is directly related to the ability of the individual nurse to assess, plan, implement and evaluate care in practice. Nurses with limited theoretical and practical knowledge will be unable to learn from clinical experience, whilst nurses with theoretical knowledge but lacking the opportunity to obtain practical knowledge may find it difficult to apply academic concepts in practical settings.

Further, Karstadt (2011) believes updating theoretical knowledge (continuous professional development) should be followed with practical knowledge gained in clinical settings to assist the nurse to attach meaning to activities and apply the learning to her/his practice. Some researchers like Rafferty, Xyrichis and Caldwell (2015) and Johnson, Hong, Groth and Parker (2011) have concluded that CPE has no impact. Others acknowledge that taught knowledge is directly related to the ability to perform in the clinical context, as experienced nurses' use different sources of knowledge to guide their practice (Brown, 2014; Cotterill-Walker, 2012; Mantzoukas and Jasper, 2008; Banning, 2008; Scott et al, 2008; Clark and Holmes, 2007). Whyte (2000) argues that having a high level of knowledge does not always translate into practical competence and the assumption that knowledge can be equated with effective performance is highly inaccurate in nursing. Integration of the theoretical and practical is a pre-requisite in clinical situations, as limited theoretical knowledge may raise difficulties in acquiring practical knowledge. On the other hand, advanced knowledge without the opportunity for experiential learning could result in an inability to apply the academic concepts or to attach meaning to activities in clinical practice. Thus, it can be argued that if taught theory is directly related to practice, nurses will be able to apply or provide relevant, safe and quality patient care.

Some question why students register on western programmes if they want to be taught in the same way as they would be in their own countries. Others ask how to contextualise theory within an unknown culture and education system.

However, Hassan (2010) assert that attempting for 'uniformity of practices' with uncritical imitation and adoption is neither practical nor desirable. This view is further highlighted by Abdullah (2010) that Malaysians who adopted and practised western values instead of integrating western ways of knowing within Malaysian values were considered by Malaysians as culturally ruthless, over-trained and brainwashed. Thus, there is need to recognise and demonstrate sensitivity by making adjustments in line with cultural conflicts to enable theoretical knowledge to be applied to practice.

Certain researchers show a dichotomy between the degree of theoretical knowledge and the ability of participants to embrace learning in their clinical settings (Schober, 2013; Leninger, 2011; Hardwick and Jordan, 2002). Generally, post-registration top-up degree programmes in the UK and Australia indicated no impact on a profession-wide improvement in practice. These findings conflict with the three studies undertaken in Malaysia (Chong, Sellick, Francis and Abdullah, 2011; Birks, 2006; Chiu, 2005). The perceived positive effect of the knowledge gained was application of knowledge in practice, and an enhancement of nurses' professional practice that resulted in improved patient care delivery. With regards to the TNHE programmes, the key factors are to identify whether the western theoretical knowledge taught has been grasped, is relevant to the wide range of settings in which nurses' work, and is applied in a meaningful way within patient care in clinical settings. In short, as Burton (2009) points out, nurse education from an international perspective needs to continue to develop standards related to evidence that is transferable across the international context.

Professional attitudes and tension

In Malaysia, the move to upgrade diploma qualifications to degree level was to meet the demands of changing nurse education, health care worldwide and to meet Vision 2020. Instead it has led to challenges within the nursing profession and work environment as some people are anti-university education, others are anti-western top-up degrees and many are against degrees that develop only western academic knowledge instead of enhancing local hands-on caring skills (Gould, Drey and Berridge, 2007; Cooley, 2008). Nursing colleagues in Malaysia who did not have a degree, or who have contempt for education or are disinterested in furthering their studies, tend to inhibit changes suggested or implemented by those who do have degrees. This is because they have concerns about their own futures and fear they will be forced to study, and of the resulting changes to their routine practices (Chong, Sellick, Francis and Abdullah, 2011; Hassan, 2010; Esmond and Sandwich, 2004). Also, there could be professional jealousy, as they perceive colleagues who have completed degree programmes have enhanced chances of promotion (Chong, Francis, Cooper and Abdullah, 2014; Chong, 2013).

These attitudes can result in reactions that range from indifference to being defensive and showing resistance and hostility. In addition, they quote that they are the real nurses as they provide hands-on care in comparison to degree qualified nurses who are considered academic nurses. Succinctly, there is a perception that studying and caring are dichotomous (Bowers, 2009; Lowe, 2003; Hardwick and Jordan, 2002) which is disputed by Hunt's (2013), Birks, Chapman and Francis' (2009b) and Girot's (2000) research that show the provision of patient care by nurses with degrees is the same or of better quality. These unsupportive and antagonistic behaviours cause tensions and leave those who study angry and frustrated. This impacts on their motivation and keenness to apply taught theory in practice post-course. It has been posited that for behavioural change in practice settings, there must be support from managers and colleagues (Gribben, McLellan and McGirr, 2017; Cotterill-Walker, 2012; McHugh and Lake, 2010; Maben, Latter and Clark, 2006; Dugdall, 2009).

Cultural impacts on TNHE teaching, learning and practice

What is culture? Hofstede (1984: 51) defined culture as the *"collective programming of the mind which distinguishes the members of one category of people from another"*. In terms of his work on understanding cultures, Hofstede (1984) explained that members of a community were regulated by behavioural patterns (influenced by upbringing and socialisation within a society) towards a situation based on beliefs (conscious or unconscious thought), norms (socially accepted rules) and values (willingness to conform to rules) learnt throughout their lives. Like Hall (1976), Hofstede concluded that culture is a pattern of thought, emotions and behaviour that is learnt, not innate, inter-connected or shared within a group. It differentiates each group in terms of their relationships with the environment, people and God, such that it becomes a way of life.

Supporting literature reveals development around his perspective and framework. It has been used extensively by Malaysian scholars (Sumaco, Imrie and Hussain, 2014; Bakar and Mustaffa, 2013; Wan Husin, 2011; Wan Yusoff, 2011; Amir, 2009; Zawawi, 2008), and by foreign researchers studying Malaysia (Ota, McCann and Honeycutt, 2012; Selvarajah and Meyer, 2008; Fontaine and Richardson, 2005). If Hofstede was right then this study of 'TNHE programming' is also part of what Hofstede refers to as a collective – where the collective is comprised of the relevant stakeholders, in this case the Malaysian Ministry of Health, MNB, TNHE providers and academics and Malaysian nurses. Already, it is clear that this collective is not a clearly defined category of people, nor is it a mind-set. The difficulty of Hofstede's thinking and his reductionism are further compounded by post-worldwide web developments accompanied by unprecedented global movements of people, information and education. Thus, the interplay between cultures represented in a TNHE classroom is what defines that culture at that moment in unique ways.

Hall (1976) believed we pick up certain beliefs and behaviours through our daily existence, and not specifically because our parents or other people have explicitly told us to do them. Hence, Tuohy (1999) points out, culture itself is not static nor a single entity, but rather multiple factors that change as the world changes and evolves through different environments and interactions. He adds that there is a continual borrowing and integration of cultural aspects between and amongst cultures; neither is any culture more superior or better equipped than others (Hall, 1976). It is therefore pointless to compare cultures since cultures are rarely formed in relation to others (Fiske, 1989). This is true. It is only when such cultures do come together, as happened in the TNHE classroom, that comparison arises showing how culture is being negotiated through underlying cultural relationships, particularly in terms of culturally understood power relationships.

Thus, it is here that Kramsch's (2017: 10) definition of culture is selected as the most viable for this research into clinical outcomes of the encounter with TNHE for Malaysian nurses. He defines culture as *"membership in a discourse community"*. In this study, that discourse community occurs in the TNHE classroom and is the major focus of the investigation. If this is so, then these Malaysian nurses enrolling in TNHE programmes with different cultural backgrounds from the dominant UK or Australian culture may have different expectations of what nursing actually is.

This is because the above theorists predict that this will have an impact on individual behaviours – in this case in clinical practice after the TNHE encounter. Kramsch, for example, believes that when a person moves into a new community such as that found in the TNHE 'collective' or 'category' (Hofstede, 1984) then they might find it difficult to give up their previously constructed perceptions of self or to digress from or relinquish certain entrenched cultural perceptions, beliefs and behaviour to adapt to the new culture. When Kramsch talks about perception of self, we can take into account for this study that self-perception amongst nurses, which arises from their socio-economic backgrounds, is just one amongst many other aspects contributing to their constructed self-perceptions. It is in this sense that this study attends to Kramsch's view, that a person may intentionally not want to break through cultural constraints to integrate new values into his or her ingrained and learnt cultural programming (Hofstede, 1984). This study, whilst recognising the complexity of multiple factors contributing to the construction of individual identities, focuses on learner identities as mediated specifically by national cultural affiliations.

To compare and understand cultures requires an insight of the interpersonal relationships that are significant to the individuals in the cultures under study. This varies between different national cultures. Also, it can be argued that as behaviour varies in different cultures, people do not react to a situation but rather to its perceived meaning. It is influenced by their national ingrained and learnt values. Kramsch's view is supported by the wide variety of generic and nursing-specific research on the experiences of international students in western universities (Lewin, 2010; Jeffreys, 2012).

Amongst the difficulties faced were language, accent of themselves and academics, western colloquialisms, new terminology or jargon, different pedagogical cultures and learning styles. Students' beliefs in the high status of western academics also affected their classroom behaviour. In practice, language difficulties affected communication and understanding of instruction given. There were challenges to assimilate and accept the western ways of care giving, and the reconciliation of cultural values and beliefs related to nursing in a different context. In addition, making sense of their learning and adjusting to different expectations of what nursing is within the HE and health care system had impacted on the integration of taught theory in clinical practice (Ling, Mazzolini and Giridharan, 2014; Bridges, 2013; Johnson, Hong, Groth and Parker, 2011; Dugdall, 2009). Beyond that there are difficulties with Kramsch's definition of culture as the same elements of reductionism arise.

Intercultural versus multicultural

Interculturalism is explained by Wright, Singh and Race (2012) as the way in which multiple cultures come together around a common purpose to promote belonging, including the pedagogy of citizenship education as policy, pedagogy and everyday practice demands. In contrast, Olson and Kraeger (2001: 116) define multiculturalism as *"when we encounter people of different culture, we discover differences in perspectives, behaviours, and communication styles"*. Succinctly, *"interculturalism is dialogical and unifying whilst multiculturalism is fragmenting"* (Carr, 2012 in Wright et al, 2012: 278). As both are useful, it is pertinent to integrate both within domestic and international education (Race, 2011). At this point, Hofstede's five notions (1991) of power distance, uncertainty avoidance, individualism-collectivism, masculinity-femininity and long-term orientation versus short-term orientation need to be revisited. These are useful notions that would help anticipate key issues in the analysis of Malaysian learner culture in relation to the TNHE programmes content and delivery.

Power distance

Power distance is described by Hofstede (1991) as acceptance or non-acceptance of power inequality in society. Malaysia is a hierarchical society, where possession of power is considered an exclusive right (c.f. Hashim and Abas, 2000). Orders given by leaders and elders or those perceived to have authority and status are in general accepted without explicit questioning. Ahmad, Shah and Aziz (2005) and Jedin and Saad (2006) agree that individualism and freedom are considered to be disrespectful as they tend to challenge authoritative views.

Abdullah (2010) and Abdullah and Koh (2009) identify teaching and learning as transference with the teacher providing the knowledge, which is enhanced by textbooks, and the students absorbing this knowledge. This didactic and hierarchical teaching method with passive learners who are trained in rote, memorisation and an exam-oriented mode of learning remained the educational model in Malaysia (Juhary, 2007; Abdullah and Pedersen, 2003).

Overall, some Malaysian scholars still deny the passive, silent, rote learners labels that characterise the students as surface learners, whilst others acknowledge these learning behaviours; but some stress that western approaches to learning are preferred (Mustapha and Abdul Rahman, 2011; Jedin and Saad, 2006; Ahmad, Shah and Aziz, 2005). The western model is considered to be more critical, where the teacher is thought to facilitate on how to access all knowledge and how to evaluate or critique it.

Although there is no *"general agreement between academics across disciplines in regards to what they believe critical thinking is"* (Egege and Kutieleh, 2004: 79), the assumption is that critical thinking is desirable, beneficial, attainable and universally valued as it is seen as the *"epitome of good thinking"* (ibid). Importantly, this is based on the 'I' (self-esteem, assertiveness and achievement) orientation of the west (Cohen and Gunz, 2002) and so there is tension with Durkin's (2004) assessment of Malaysian culture as non-individualistic and harmony-seeking.

Although the Malaysia Plan, with a Vision for 2020, aims for a learner-centred approach to replace the traditional didactic approach, the movement away from the traditional mode is hampered by culturally entrenched rules (c.f. Abdullah, 2010).

Whilst Hofstede (1980) maintained there was a culture and tradition of obedience to authority in Malaysia, twenty years later Durkin (2004) posits instead the importance of Malaysians' valuing social harmony. It was identified that one of the aims of education in Malaysia was to contribute to the harmony and betterment of the family, society and country. I also point out that the power distance has an impact on the educational styles. Interestingly, the Malaysian national education philosophy was influenced by western educational philosophies rather than indigenous concepts. But, the present colonial-influenced educational system is considered eastern by the western world (MoHE, 2010; Birks, 2007).

Asian students are challenged when they face the western academic style that is considered to be of a high status as it emphasises self-directed learning, problem solving, analytical skills and critical enquiry (Mok, 2013; Arif, Ilyas and Hameed, 2013; Chuang, 2012; Gill, 2009). If western critical thinking skills are a pre-requisite, how they are to be taught is relevant to this study, in particular as Samuelowicz (1987: 124) stated, *"the intellectual skills of comparing, evaluating different points of view, arguing and presenting one's point of view are not developed"*. This is because the critical thinking model would need to be used by nurses to internalise and contextualise the evidence base for their clinical settings.

Uncertainty avoidance

This is the extent to which members of a culture *"feel threatened by uncertain or unknown situations"*. They may feel uncomfortable and ambiguous, but attempt to navigate around it by recognising how much they share in common with different others (Hofstede, 2001: 113). The diverse ethnic groups Bumiputeras (a term used for Malaysians of indigenous Malay origin), Chinese, Indians, Eurasians, Tamils, Babas, Portugese and Dutch in Malaysia each have their own language, religious traditions and customs that have been learned and passed down from one generation to another. Abdullah and Pedersen (2003) use the term *multicultural parallelism* to describe this situation. Extensive variation is evident in Malaysian society with regard to the behaviour patterns of each ethnic group and their preference to retain their own identity, religion, custom, social practices and tradition. As a range of ethnic groups is represented in the TNHE programmes, this study will focus only on the set of shared patterns where they influence beliefs, norms and values, i.e. particular sensitivity to shame, maintenance of face (self-esteem), defensiveness of one's own face or that of elders or people in authority or power, respect for people with higher status, and westerners. Showing confidence overtly or displaying assertive behaviour is likely to be frowned upon and confrontation is avoided (Abdullah, 2010; Jedin and Saad, 2006; Hashim and Abas, 2000).

These writers go on to claim that in interpersonal relationships, tolerance is valued amongst and between ethnic groups. This naive final claim is in itself face-saving for the national culture. It is considered polite not to express potentially negative views, therefore feelings are selectively articulated. Abdullah (2010) points out that being outspoken and being articulate are not distinguished from each other in Malaysian culture. The indication here is that speaking individually or privately is likely to be preferred over speaking publicly so to avoid the risk of humiliating oneself or hurting others' feelings. Shared patterns due to intrinsic cultural traditions in Malaysians are known as part of the 'we' (face, modesty and harmony) orientation (Cohen and Gunz, 2002), which is corroborated by Mohamad (2008), whose own view, even as he stresses the perceived negativity and harm in the frankness of westerners, is that it is valuable and Malaysians need to adopt it for their own progress.

Asian cultural values have been explored extensively in the literature (Jin and Cortazzi, 2013a and b; Mustapha and Nik Abdul Rahman, 2011; Heffernan, Morrison, Basu and Sweeney, 2010; Hassan and Jamaludin, 2010), but in Langguth's *Asian Values Revisited* (2003), he questions the validity of these perceptions being attributed to Asian values. He argues that when multi-ethnic, multi-cultural and multi-faiths are involved, what is clear is that Asian values are opposite to western values and ideas (Mohamad, 2008).

Individualism-collectivism

Cultural dimensions of individualism-collectivism have been used to refer to a person's relationship to the group, and to characterise varying beliefs, norms and social values to illuminate and explain differences in behaviour among cultures (Triandis, 1995). Normally, western cultures are classified as individualist and described as autonomous and independent, whilst eastern cultures are termed collectivistic due to individuals deriving their identity from their role within the community (Fiske, 1989). This dichotomy of each cultural orientation at opposite ends of a continuum has been rejected. Not all individualist cultures engage in low-context interaction that is straightforward, explicit and self-serving. Neither do all collectivistic cultures have high context communication that is indirect and implicit (Hall, 1976).

In addition, with the present global environment, no country has a single or homogeneous individualist or collectivist culture. Instead, it is multidimensional; personal characteristics, communication styles and preferences from both individualistic and collectivistic structures are used in different situations (Dema and Moeller, 2012). What is evident is that all cultures share human mentality (Hofstede, 1980), emotional belief systems (Trice and Beyer, 1993), value systems (Turner and Trompenaars, 1993) and behaviour (Harris, 1968) within their different perspectives and meanings.

In relation to TNHE programmes, it is important to recognise that Malaysian society is defined as vertical collectivism (Abdullah, 2010; Hassan, 2010; Abdullah and Koh, 2009; Abdullah and Pedersen, 2003) due to the expectation that orders given by powerful leaders and those perceived to have authority are accepted without question. These are developed in parallel with the domain (identity defined by shared interest), community (learn from each other but not always working together on a daily basis) and practice (shared resources of experiences and problem solving). As nurses are represented from a range of ethnic groups in this study, it is vital to point out that the strength of the cultural values of collectivism and power has a slight variance within each ethnic group. However, nurses' classroom interaction and experiences may be dictated by their different communal values, beliefs and behaviour patterns or shared patterns as these are ingrained and often acted out unconsciously.

Hence, it is pertinent for western academics to recognise and gain understanding to ensure that appropriate strategies are used to mitigate misunderstandings in the teaching and learning process and classroom management. This is to facilitate the application of theoretical knowledge in practice.

Masculinity-femininity

Opportunities for men and women differ in Malaysian society with men generally being privileged and having more power than the submissive women. In recent years, the Malaysian government's position has appeared to promote greater gender equality as it signed the Putrajaya Declaration at the Non-Aligned Movement (NAM) Ministerial Meeting on the Advancement of Women (1995).

Changing the way gender roles and power relations are enacted requires challenging long-held and deeply ingrained societal beliefs about the role of women in Malaysia, especially when cultural, religious and traditional practices remain influential in dictating the role, image and privileges of women in society.

With most societies, the role, status and positioning of nursing is a clear reflection of global factors that influence all nurses, i.e. women's work, image and stereotype. In some countries including Malaysia, nurses also have to contend with traditional structures and oppression due to religion, tradition, cultural and institutional barriers (Abdullah, 2010; Birks, Chapman and Francis, 2009a; Bryant, 2017; Ministry of Women, Family and Community Development, 2004). This has resulted in the perception that nursing is a female profession and a menial task (Alexander, 2010). Thus, in Malaysia, there are only 361 male nurses in comparison with the 67,988 female nurses (International Council of Nurses, 2008).

Long-term versus short term orientation

Long-term orientation was formerly known as *Confucian dynamism* as it looks at the extent to which a society maintains traditional values (Hofstede, 2001). There is a tendency for an eastern country like Malaysia to ascribe to the values of long-term commitment and respect for tradition; so in relation to work, long-term rewards are expected. In contrast, employees in western countries expect short-term rewards from their work. It can be argued that even within a culture like Malaysia's, there are certain ethnic groups that prefer short term commitment whilst others prefer long term commitment.

In relation to the TNHE classroom environment, it was relevant to consider the significant insights and cultural perceptions between Malaysian cultural rules and the western context using Hofstede's dimensions. It allowed exploration to enable awareness and insight. As both the western academics and nurses may have their own assumptions and expectations about the nature of their world and others' worlds, the only way this context may be communicated is via interpersonal interactions. If this is not achieved, the extensive variation may result in shock at the new teaching and learning environment. Having understood the cultural values of Malaysians, readers will be able to understand the potential impact that TNHE experiences may have on the nurses and their behaviour.

Culture shock and learning shock

The term *culture shock* was first defined by Kalervo Oberg (1960: 68), an anthropologist working in the 1950's. He defined culture shock as:

"precipitated by the anxiety that results from losing all our familiar signs and symbols of social intercourse. These signs or cues include the thousand and one ways in which we orient ourselves to the situations of daily life".

Davidson (2013) believes that, as culture shock applies to any new situation, relationship, job or perspective, people will assume their way of thinking or behaving is the only way and is correct human nature. Often they are unaware of having learnt their cultural ways or how much it shapes their attitudes towards time, space and interpersonal communication. Initial shock may be replaced by the inspiration to self-reflect.

The literature on culture shock in HE is focused on international students leaving their own country and travelling to study at a university in another country (UKCISA, 2008; Griffiths, Winstanley and Gabriel, 2004, Robertson, 2000). Only recently has the literature started to focus on home international students (c.f. Pyvis and Chapman, 2005). The phenomena relating to culture shock, specifically to the academic context, is learning shock (Davidson, 2013; Ballard and Clanchy, 1997), study shock (Knox, 2000; Burns, 1991), cognitive dissonance (Furnham, 2004; Festinger, 1957), and intellectual culture shock (Currie, and Knights, 2003; Ballard, 1987). These describe the experience of acute frustration, conflict, disbelief and disorientation experienced by students when exposed to new teaching and learning methods. Irrespective of whether the students travel to another country or are in their home country, the unexpected and different cues that are difficult to decode, familiar signs which harbour unfamiliar meanings, conflicting expectations, cultural and learning clashes, especially in the university context, affect the students psychologically and emotionally with implications for their coping strategies (Ryan and Hellmundt, 2003). The level of emotional disturbance varies from individual to individual based on their previous experiences, preparation for the new environment and their expectations.

The TNHE top-up degree programmes are still quite new in Malaysia and are provided to nurses who would be returning to study after a protracted absence from academia. Previous research has shown the shock reactions of adults and mature students when they return to education after many years, based on their earlier experiences (Griffiths, Winstanley and Gabriel, 2004; Pyvis and Chapman, 2005). They relied on proven routines, methods and memory to pass examinations and may now find the diversity of teaching methods and learning styles distressing (Sadler-Smith, 2001). A fear of failure and a lack of confidence in their ability with academic writing skills may also result in feelings of insecurity and inadequacy (Chasseguet-Smirgel, 1976). But often they are committed and work hard to transform their previous learnt or existing beliefs to integrate new learning (Hellsten and Prescott, 2004; Levy, Osborn, and Plunkett, 2003) to make it more satisfying in its achievements. Cross-cultural adjustment or adaptation is required to engage in a new academic environment or learning culture.

From shock to adjustment, or adaptation to transformation

Many theoretical models have been developed to capture the nature and process of adjustment or adaptation and have been described and measured in varying ways and from several perspectives. Although there is no consensus on a single definition or clarity of what adjustment or adaptation means, I have chosen to use the construct from Anderson (1994) as it refers to adjustment as a process that happens between an individual and the new environment. In contrast, adaptation is directed towards a psychological and socio-cultural achievement of fit between the individual and the new learning culture (Anderson, 1994). The difference between the two concepts as succinctly explained by Shaffer and Shoben (1956, cited in Anderson, 1994) is that adjustment is related to short-term encounters whilst adaptation is useful for long-term survival. Whilst it clearly reveals the differences, according to Savicki et al (2008) appraisal and coping strategies of individuals are related to both adjustments and adaptations along a continuum as they exhibit varying degrees and modes of adjustment or adaptation when faced with situations in the new environment.

People have little control over inherited characteristics and when they assimilate into a culture, group members expect them to observe, learn, adopt and conform to the social beliefs, norms, values, self-identity and behavioural responses of that culture (Dumont, 1986). Members of the culture define and describe themselves with the internal reality gained through years of socialising experiences. This affirmed and reinforced knowledge that has become their way of life is shared with new members.

Thus, both adjustment and adaptation require a conscious learning process as initial emotions and thoughts generate responses that usually result in 'flight or fight' reactions to new ways. A person may adjust quickly. Over time, as the person continues to face these differences, they will learn and become accustomed to the ways of the new culture and thus will 'adapt' to cultural differences. The key is that it requires a gradual transition as people move from a state of familiarity to unfamiliarity when immersed in a new environment over a long period of time (Shakya and Horsfall, 2000; Sanner, 2002).

Kim (1988) in her stress-adaptation-growth model identified two key trends in reviewing adaptation processes, i.e. problem-oriented perspective, such as culture shock studies, and learning and growth outlook. These demonstrate the intercultural learning experience as a transitional experience reflecting movement from low self- and cultural-awareness to high self- and cultural-awareness. According to Kim and Ruben (1988: 299), from a social psychological perspective, an integrative model of intercultural transformation focuses on the internal change process where *"individual's cognitive, affective and behavioural patterns develop beyond their original culturally conditioned psychological parameters"*.

Intercultural identity was later referred to by Kim (2001) as an acquired identity, by Grotevant (1992) as adopted identity and by Phinney (1993 cited in Kim, 2001: 191) as achieved identity. The development of intercultural identity is a stress-adaptation-growth process (Kim, 1992) that indicates it is not static, but the strain and pressure to comply may lead to change in one's intercultural identity. When individuals mix with members of other cultural groups, they adjust to different identities utilising integration strategies by blending important aspects of both cultures. Kim's assumption was also that maintaining cultural ties and communication with the originating culture will interfere with the adaptation process as it may highlight the incompatibility with one's own values or traditions. This makes adaptation difficult. So, often a person will add valuable resources to their original cultural resources rather than relinquish these original attributes. The adjustment process to the new environment improves the longer individuals reside in the new environment (c.f. Wilton and Constantine, 2003).

Most studies focus on Asian students from a traditional collectivist culture that is more didactic, structured and hierarchical with educational success measured by ability to reproduce knowledge. On transfer to the individualistic culture of western HE, these students were challenged by their language ability, learning styles, academic study skills and pedagogical cultures (c.f. Furnham, 1997). In addition, the HEIs' inability to provide sufficient support, contributes to stress (Kirby, Knapper, Evans, Carty, and Gadula, 2003). Despite this, transformation of self was recognised with improved confidence that may be due to the sense of achievement (Wang, 2010).

I argue that even when one moves to a new environment or another country, it is difficult and it takes time to accept different cultural rules, let alone to internalise changes when one remains in one's own country (Ryan and Hellmundt, 2003; Chapman and Pyvis, 2005). This complexity is also highlighted by my experiences as an international student nurse. In this regard the difference between adjusting as a survival strategy and adapting in terms of cultural negotiation are discussed.

In relation to my study, I argue that in consideration of the nature of TNHE programmes that involve a short one- or two-week period of face-to-face or on-line study undertaken every semester over two years, the tendency is for these nurses to be adjusters rather than adaptors. Despite a shared code of professional values and behaviour, the differences in language or culture in the classroom, educational and health care, may cause communication barriers. This is because Malaysians have a strong and well-defined set of cultural values which may affect how nursing students adjust to western cultural rules. Not all will follow or practice these values. The tendency for nurses in this study may be to adjust to meet the assessment criteria and achieve their degrees. However, for TNHE learning which focuses on the professional ideals of the western world to have an impact, and for the knowledge to be integrated, accepted and sustained in practice settings, these nurses would need to make adaptations rather than adjustments. This would take time. They would need to reflect on their values and beliefs when they are initially faced with unfamiliar teaching and learning experiences.

Effective coping strategies would need to be used. Individuals will have to use their own resources to cope with the challenges they face, whilst also appreciating and integrating new cultural practices into their own resources. Further, to understand the complexity of the nurses' adaptation, an integrated perspective involving intellectual, personal, social and practical changes must be considered. It is also important to point out that an overall picture of what is important in society as a whole may affect adaptation. In relation to my study, the adjustment and adaptation aspects are pertinent as they will identify the nurses' learning in line with their previous nurse educational experiences.

Adjustment towards change from TNHE teaching and learning

My study aims to identify whether TNHE theoretical knowledge has changed Malaysian nurses' personal and professional selves to enable implementation of such knowledge in clinical practice whilst also coping with others' acceptance to change. Change is movement away from a present state toward a new way (Gorg, 2013) or a response to some significant threat or opportunity arising outside of the organization (Hellsten and Prescott (2004). It has been pointed out that values within oneself must change to enable a shift in belief (conscious or unconscious thought a person holds) and attitudes (beliefs influenced by upbringing and socialisation in a society) that are displayed by behaviour (invoked from memory based on knowledge and experiences) towards a situation (Sampath, Bankwala and Sampath, 2006). As values are learned preferences that provide standards against which people act and events can be judged, they tend to change as the environment changes. But sometimes people prefer to maintain values despite pressure to change as they find it challenging to adapt to a new context that places greater stress (Kim, 2001) on them. For example, in my study the stressors could be the self-directed learning, problem solving and critical analysis.

Acquisition of knowledge and competence in a foreign language is:

> "not an evolutionary improvement on what precedes it; rather, new knowledge enter adversarial relationships with older, more established ones, challenging their position in the power play of understandings, and in such confrontations new insights can be provoked" (Fiske, 1989: 194 cited in Kramsch, 2017: 238).

As people struggle or are confronted with unfamiliar ways in the educational process of the intercultural encounter, it leads to change (Kramsch, 2017). It would appear that after an initial culture shock and acculturation period, students adjust and begin to appreciate their increased independence, freedom and responsibility.

Discussion of the literature

In this chapter, literature related to the research questions and issues examined during the study have been presented. TNHE and the new developments in HE share certain common characteristics, mainly in terms of the way they cross the borders of national HE, and are thus identified by the generic phrase of TNHE. Knight (2004) believed that a rational application of the definition of TNHE will exclude twinning, joint degrees and credit transfer programmes. In reality, the Australian definition of education and training offered in international education (onshore), distance mode (offshore) and virtual or distance or e-learning delivered without a physical presence of instructors, should not be regarded as part of TNHE education and training. Their definition does not apply because western HEIs are non-specific.

These contradictory definitions have led to terminological and conceptual confusion as a variety of relationships, types of providers, delivery, mechanisms, and programmes and awards are continually developed to reflect the individual institution's directions and trends. Despite their differences, the different forms of programmes discussed earlier are components of an international education system, with different emphasis on the mobility of people, programmes or HEIs. Further, there has been a rise in unscrupulous providers of TNHE who promise quick returns, degree mills (web-based companies selling certificates based on life experiences with non-delivery of educational programmes) and rogue providers selling bogus qualifications. It has caused mayhem for international qualification recognition (Garrett, 2015).

It has been argued that the UK and Australian TNHE exporting countries appear to have failed to adopt a planned approach that relates to the needs and demands of a specific country (Leask and Carroll, 2011; Knight, 2011; Smith, 2009). As I highlighted in an example in Chapter I, there are TNHE universities that teach off-the-shelf modules with minimum changes made to meet the needs of the Malaysian nurses. Whilst this appears to be a blatant commercialisation of an existing educational programme and is disrespectful to the students (Leask and Carroll, 2011; Knight, 2008; Dunn and Wallace, 2008), it also shows cultural values that affect culturally influenced behaviour have not been considered. It leads to what Ziguras (2016), Caruana and Montgomery (2015) and Garrett (2015) describe as teaching down to communities that are culturally different from that of the teachers. Garrett (2015) also argues that it demonstrates colonialism and commoditisation of education with low quality standardised packages of information.

There is a need to recognise and demonstrate sensitivity by making adjustments to the programmes in line with cultural issues, to enable application of knowledge gained to practice (Cathro, 2011) as offshore teaching is both an intense intercultural and educational encounter (Leask and Caroll, 2011). This is evident from Fitch and Surma's (2006) view that, in their keenness as academics trying to achieve equivalence in learning outcomes, their assumptions had been that their teaching and learning approach will automatically be understood by TNHE students. Only later did they recognise that students' cultural and educational experiences meant they had different expectations. However, the constraints of institutional processes and practices had prevented them from making the required adjustments crucial to developing a genuinely international approach. Offshore teaching requires more than delivering all the material in the textbook or providing a course identical to the one being offered at the home campus (Ziguras, 2016). Biggs (2014) argues that these students have been identified as seeking a western education, and whilst Ziguras and McBurnie (2015) agree, they argue that the exporting universities' concern is quality assurance and standardisation; hence, the same education is delivered to all students. Dunn and Wallace (2008) state that the assumption of TNHE providers is that 'one size fits all'.

Nurse education in the early years was similar within each of the three countries discussed here, with nursing skills acquired through hospital-based training. Although nurse education to Diploma level was transferred to HE, such as degree programmes for both the UK and Australia, in Malaysia, diploma nursing remains hospital-based with limited numbers of universities providing degree programmes. As nursing is a practice discipline, all three countries emphasise CPD/CPE/MCPE as a professional requirement for nurses. This is to ensure the continued updating of their knowledge and skills to ensure competent, relevant and quality patient care.

Chong (2013), Cotterill-Walker (2012), Chiu (2006) and Birks (2005) believe post-registration courses in nurse education must enable academic skills and knowledge to develop from and underpin nursing practice, especially in the national context. This will enable the nurses to make links to assess, plan, implement and evaluate directly or indirectly, to improve patient care in the multi-ethnic, multi-cultural and multi-lingual dimensions of Malaysian society.

The establishment of top-up degree programmes leading to registration provided the option for nurses with diplomas to upgrade their qualifications. The literature shows that those who chose this option usually had both professional and personal motives, seeking to keep up to date, to advance their careers and to gain personal achievement. Also evident from the literature was that having support and coping mechanisms was crucial to surviving the journey, as they face challenges such as returning to education with added family responsibility and lack of workplace support. The effects and outcomes of having a degree were usually considered from a personal, rather than a wider professional outlook, leaving another gap in the literature. It was also evident that, whilst information on motives, barriers, support and outcomes for undertaking top-up degree exists, the country-specific contexts also had an influence.

Sturdy and Gabriel (2000) and Knight (2004) point out that resistance to western practices in Malaysia is due to former colonial status, whilst Juhary (2007) argues that it is due to keenness to construct a unifying national identity and culture to support economic growth and political stability among ethnic groups. Cross-cultural issues usually arise when shifting from an open western environment to a more traditional eastern background, and cultural adaptation or adjustment is required (Hunt, 2013). Kim (2001) argued that cross-cultural adaptation is a lifelong process. Yang's 2006 study (cited in Huang, 2006) notes western TNHE providers or programmes may have an impact both educationally and culturally on the students, to shape their identities towards western values, but education is influenced by the national cultures of both providers and students.

An international perspective recognises the movement of people and information that embraces another's cultural space. It cannot be assumed that both cultures share similar contexts, meaning and application of the teaching and learning experience. Now, more and more western HEIs (Lynch, 2013; United Kingdom Council for International Student Affairs, 2008) are starting to recognise Ryan's (2011) view that they cannot expect eastern students to conform to western models of education. It is due to the different influences of race and culture on perceptions and beliefs in education as Abdullah

(2010) and Hassan (2010) assert that attempting for uniformity of practices with uncritical imitation and adoption is neither practical nor desirable.

Research on overseas students is now extensive and focuses on difficulties they face, stages and factors that influence their adjustment and adaptations (or not), (Gaw, 2000). Since the 1990s there has been a shift in theorising the interface of learning and culture. Culture influences learning, but learning itself is a process of transformation as patterns of social interaction, insight of the world and cognitive capabilities are challenged. Learners use their learnt values to make sense of their world but the learners' engagement and participation in new activities often result in re-learning, modifying and creating new cultural outlooks. The willingness to learn and adapt is necessary when one faces a new context, especially when it takes place between societies with differing cultures, political systems and levels of economic development.

Consideration of the cultural perceptions of Malaysians will act as a foundation to facilitate appropriate teaching, uptake of learning and provision of culturally competent care. Failure to recognise, understand and respect culturally sensitive ingrained language and traditions of each ethnic group, education and health care system when teaching nurses may also have implications on the theory-practice connection.

The impact of cultural differences on learning outcomes was explored by Leask and Carroll (2011) whose findings indicated the curriculum must be adapted to local needs. This is also supported by Leininger (2011). Further, Biggs (2014) stresses the importance of considering students' prior learning in curricular development and teaching practices. The emphasis should be on balance between integrating social, cultural, educational needs to ensure what is taught has relevance to the students and the same quality assurance of western educational programmes (Jin and Cortazzi, 2011a&b). The aims of TNHE programmes should be to broaden students' frames of reference, facilitate them to internalise the practices of the new culture of learning and/or mediate between and mobilise the two learning cultural resources. This in effect means to create new forms of learning to enable them to embrace these practices within their prior learning. This has brought its own set of difficulties.

Many UK and Australian universities began their TNHE collaborations with distance education programmes designed for their local students (Ziguras, 2016). It appears only limited consideration has been given to the UNESCO and OECD (2005:14) *Guidelines for Quality Provision in Cross-Border Higher Education* that state awarding institutions should:

> "Ensure that the programmes they deliver across borders and in their home country are of comparable quality and that they also take into account the cultural and linguistic sensitivities of the receiving country. It is desirable that a commitment to this effect should be made public."

This refrain that TNHE provision is mainly a commercial exchange rather than an integration of international educational, cultural and social endeavour questions their appropriateness. Also questionable is their quality, applicability and effectiveness to meet the human resource needs of Malaysia's national economy, as outlined in Vision 2020, the national plans and the industrial master plans. It also highlights that as acquiring cultural values is tacit, and even problematic as it involves intellectual humility and cognitive endeavour, TNHE providers prefer to reflect their individual HEIs' directions and particular trends in their own internationalisation strategies (Knight and Morshidi, 2011; Leask and Carroll, 2011).

There is a general belief that TNHE programmes are protected by national regulations and a variety of standards and codes of practice, it thought critical that the curricula of TNHE programmes are similar to those delivered in the home country, with suitable revisions made to suit the student group and the local context (Bennett et al., 2010). This notion appears straight forward. In reality, there are challenges to conform to different regulatory frameworks of collaborating countries, partly, because of the difficulty of ascertaining the degree of similarity or difference between programmes. This is due to the educational, language and cultural variations where the TNHE programmes are delivered. In short, there is no one-size-fits-all model of quality assurance. This may be contributing to evidence that some TNHE providers avoid aspects of the national accreditation restrictions of the countries receiving these programmes (Ziguras, 2016; Bennett et al., 2010). This is discussed further in this book. It has led to the potential mismatch between programme contents and host country's social norms and regulations (Smith, 2009). This in turn does not enhance the global, international and intercultural student experience nor does it demonstrate TNHE programmes are credible or that their credentials are internationally recognised. What seems apparent is that TNHE providers' opportunistic programme developments are income generating in the short-term but may not be sustainable long-term as their quality assurance systems are ad hoc and reactive in manner.

Chapter 3. Revealing my roles and stances

In this research, I used reflexivity in an attempt to unravel, examine and illustrate my personal, professional and researcher roles. I questioned the need to narrate my personal story when the research was about the experience of others. To me, writing the personal 'I' appeared to be confessional, used to make explicit to the reader that thoughts about my experiences were important and interesting to be presented within an academic work.

But, reflexivity, as Skeggs (2002) explains, is more than simply the telling of the self or writing a paragraph about self in a research text. These types of gestures assume that by adding a piece about the self, the problems of power, perspective and privilege are dissolved. In reality, "selfing" (Skeggs, 2002: 360) or "what counts as evidence" (Skeggs, 2002: 349) is used to reflect critically on one's identity and feelings and lived experiences in order to share experiences. Skeggs' thoughts were similar to Wenger's (1998) in that, speaking and writing about familiar lived experiences provides opportunities to explore, examine and rethink those experiences. These arguments were considered when adopting the strategies throughout the research process.

Personal reflexivity

Personal reflexivity involves reflecting on one's "values, norms and concepts that have been assimilated during a lifetime" (Denscombe, 2007: 333). It provides "a public account of the self which explores the role of the researcher self" (Denscombe, 2007: 69) to declare the "authority used to claim knowledge" (Fox, 1999: 220). I included aspects of my own past and present self, the previous 'me' and the current 'I', but not my future self.

Despite Parker's (1999: 92) warning to avoid the "spiral of passivity" that focuses only towards certain painful explanations, and Skeggs' (2002: 360) emphasis of "indulging in a fascination with self", I reflected to identify certain relevant, painful and exciting Malaysian and British experiences that had hitherto remained hidden. Engaging in on-going critical self-questioning allowed me to bring to the surface my 'taken for granted' values and assumptions. This enabled me to acknowledge and challenge them either to make new choices or to let go and make clear how I was and am positioned within my study. Although some may challenge that just because it was difficult for me to adapt to British culture, I was assuming it would be the same for these TNHE nurses. I agree but I cannot assume it.

Professional reflexivity

Professional reflexivity is recognising one's professional identity and adopting a reflexive position to examine knowledge, ideas, values, attributes, attitude and skills. Taylor and White (2000) believe it characterises the role and the self-in-role. As the identity of an individual is assessed by their behaviour within the profession, professional attributes are achieved by learning the necessary theory and skills. They are also shaped by building relationships through interactions between self and others, within and outside of the profession group, and comments from users of the service.

The impact of my personal self as a Malaysian, international student, UK resident, nurse, academic and practitioner-researcher on my research was made clear and their influences appear throughout the research. As a Malaysian, I recognise that expectations and preferences towards the provision of care in Malaysia are determined by individual ethnic groups based on traditional and non-western views. These health beliefs involve values, physical, emotional, social, political aspects and their relationship to the environment. Whilst healthcare providers in Malaysia focus on the importance of adhering to the WHO standard practices, there are also strategies in place to integrate the multicultural, multilingual and multi-ethnic patients' cultural and traditional beliefs and ways with the modern approaches of care (Ibrahim, Nik Yusoff and Kamarudin, 2016; Chee and Barraclough, 2007).

In adopting a reflexive approach, I point out that I attained my nursing qualification in the UK and worked as a nurse, nurse academic and practitioner-researcher exclusively within the UK. Hence, my memories, thoughts and viewpoints are based on the UK nurse education, healthcare delivery approaches, professional status of nurses, demands and advances. I immersed myself in UK nursing values and expectations in line with the requirements of the NMC professional body. My personal and professional self, influenced my practitioner-researcher self and my research.

Researcher reflexivity

Epistemological reflexivity encourages constant thought of the "interpretations of both our experience and the phenomena being studied so as to move beyond the partiality of our previous understandings" (Finlay, 2003: 108). My research identity was grounded in myself as a Malaysian, international student, UK resident, nurse, nurse academic and practitioner-researcher. My hidden assumptions impacted unknowingly on my research and in interpreting participants' experiences.

Researchers often position themselves as either insiders (emic) or outsiders (etic) within the qualitative research domain, to enable questioning to occur at each stage of the research process. The insider is someone whose biography (gender, race, class), gives them a lived familiarity with the cultural aspects relating to members of the group being researched. In contrast, outsiders do not share knowledge with the group, community and environment being researched. They rely on extrinsic categories and concepts prior to entry into the group (Kitzinger, 2006). Succinctly, insiders "cannot escape their past" whilst an outsider is "without a history" of the research setting (Schutz, 1964: 34).

From an interpretivist position, the social world is subjective and can only be understood from the point of view of the participants (Denzin and Lincoln, 2011). The interpretive, hermeneutic phenomenological approach informed by the ethnographic principle of cultural interpretation was selected to enable subjective viewpoints and self-reflexivity. Hermeneutics positions the researcher within the research process (van Manen, 2014), and I as the researcher was allowed to determine how my study would develop. The ethnographic principle of cultural interpretation (Agar, 2011; Geetz, 1973) enabled me to illuminate the reasons behind the nurses' views. My personal insights and viewpoints, both as a Malaysian and as a resident of the UK, privileged me, rather than introduced bias. It enabled me to consider my own biases and assumptions, to justify the reasoning behind my actions and data collection and to interpret the voices of the Malaysian nurses (van Manen, 2014; Denzin and Lincoln, 2011).

As a result, I argue against the view of the tendency unconsciously to choose what issues to pick up on, ask questions about during the interviews and put my own slant to shape the interpretation of nurses' voices. Prior to data collection, I had formulated four key aspects that would focus the interviews towards answering the aim of this study. Thus, the reader of the research is aware of them whilst I interpret the data.

Personal, professional and researcher stances

Influential personal stance

Personal stance is the position which "each of us takes up in life and our experiences that reflect its social and relational aspect" (Salmon, 1989: 231). My stance is rooted in my experiences as a Malaysian and international student nurse in the UK, and is identified below to enable the reader to capture its specific influences on the research.

When I first came to the UK, I was fascinated by all the differences in life, culture, habits, sights-sounds-smells and tastes, but soon I realised its strangeness in relation to my childhood/adult memories and experiences of being a Malaysian. My former daily life was centred within the traditions, food and religion of the Tamil culture, in the centre of other diverse ethnic groups of Malays, Chinese, Indians, Eurasians, Babas, Dutch and Portugese. Relationships between the groups are maintained by mutual respect and a shared tradition of tolerance among and between each race, which has led to Malaysia's uniquely diverse heritage.

In Malaysia, English speaking or western education is depicted as modern and prestigious. However, a post-colonial statement with regards to educational policies introduced Bahasa Malaysia, as a medium of instruction in all Malaysian schools, to replace English language. English became just a subject to study as part of the curriculum, like Geography. Now living in Britain, the threads from my own taken-for-granted childhood and adult memories that were subtle and ingrained in me, and often unconsciously applied in my everyday life, became visible to me for the first time.

Intense feelings of uncertainty arose about what was expected of me, or what to expect from others in my personal and student nurse life, due to the contrasts in many ways. This was a difficult and lonely time with painful and fearful emotions; stress and disorientation, as I grappled with my values and habitual ways of speaking, thinking and behaving as culture shock set in.

In addition, the 'tell and test' teaching approach that promoted the objective of remembering as much as possible from the teachers and textbooks in order to pass exams, was the only teaching I knew and thought existed. The demands of a British university nurse education, with a learner-centred culture where the teacher instructs how to access, evaluate or critique knowledge, were frustrating. There was a mismatch between my entrenched thoughts of 'saving face', of listening to learn and memorising, and the British approach of 'talking to learn'.

The English language as spoken in the UK was also a problem for me. Cronin and Rawlings-Anderson (2004) asserted that languages of the world differ, so societies, cultures and subgroups attach different meanings to words used in communication. My experiences indicated what Ryan (2011) described as learning shock, a difference between new modes and one's belief system of teaching and learning. I also experienced feelings of uncertainty and uneasiness, as I did not know what to say or do, due to lack of cultural knowledge.

> I remember clearly as if it had just occurred. The first time during my Diploma in Nursing, we were all given photocopies of an article and were asked 'WHAT OUR THOUGHTS WERE'. My own first thoughts were THINK! I have never had to think during my studies in Malaysia! All I used to do was listen to the teacher in class, jot down in my exercise book the key aspects relevant to the specific subject and focus on what the teacher told us was important for our examinations. When I went home, I would go through the notes, read the relevant textbooks from cover to cover and memorise the information to re-gurgitate for my exams!
>
> So, when we were put into small groups with me being the only international student in an all English group of six, I did not know what to expect. When one student had finished reading, she just started giving her opinion and others got involved either asking questions or giving their views. I had not even finished reading the article nor had I understood what I was reading!
>
> I was impressed by their highly articulate and assertive conversation but struggled to keep up with the discussion due to their accents and my own poor English and lack of subject knowledge. Only after awhile did they realise that I had not said a word! How could I! Then suddenly all attention was directed to me - What do you think? You have been very quiet! Oooo...h! I remember wishing I was not there! I SMILED, LOOKED DOWN AT THE ARTICLE and KEPT QUIET.
>
> (Reflective account: 23rd June, 2008).

I do acknowledge that these were my own feelings and shyness in relation to speaking up in class or when I entered a mixed group. I admit that another Malaysian, with a different personality and experience, may not have shared these emotions or reacted in the same way. In Malaysia, recognition of the advanced western ways of teaching and learning is respected and considered by most, if not all, as prestigious. So, I anticipated that the TNHE nurses may still have inhibitions and would have reacted in a similar way.

Writing assignments in English for the first time was a challenge, and caused anxiety, as assessment criteria, reflection, critical reasoning, referencing and plagiarism were concepts I had never heard of, nor thought about. Having come from Malaysia where I had written in the first person and in Bahasa Malaysia, I now had to learn to write academically in English and in the third person to create an illusion of objectivity. I also had to learn what being critical meant and how to be critical to add value to analysis.

Clinical learning experiences are stressful and cause anxiety to all students, but for me it was more complex. As I had arrived in the UK just in time to begin my studies, I had not had adequate time to be exposed to, or become acculturated to, the UK culture, education, healthcare system and nursing. The English language as spoken in practice settings also became a problem for me. Firstly, because of the speed at which nurses spoke; secondly, the jargon and colloquialisms used were strange; and thirdly, I translated common expressions literally. However, not all languages have direct translation of terms and even when they do exist, they are not used in the same way.

I had a range of different clinical experiences and faced a variety of situations that strengthened my identity as a student nurse as I learnt to apply the professional knowledge, skills and language taught in the classroom in practice settings. Clinical practice assessments also required the transfer of taught theory for the provision of patient care. I emphasise that the assessment criteria may have been clear and appropriate to demonstrate that theoretical and clinical learning outcomes had been achieved, but it totally baffled me as it was a new educational experience. My learning in the clinical environment was delayed by the differences between my own cultural beliefs of nursing approaches in Malaysia and UK practice settings. Nurses in TNHE programmes may face similar challenges because the education system still does not require one to write assignments, use English or have western critical and reasoning skills. The teacher and books are still considered authoritative sources of knowledge.

As nursing is a practice-based profession, the theoretical knowledge taught is developed alongside clinical practice in the academic programme all around the world (Gribben, McLellan, McGirr and Chenery-Morris, 2017; Reed, 2012; Karstadt, 2011; Dyess and Chase, 2010). Personally, I also feel that only with this theory-practice link will the student nurse be able to provide patient care in a meaningful way in either UK hospitals and/or community settings. I was aware that students who did not have the opportunity for hands-on experience found it difficult to apply their learning from the classroom in practice settings. The professional knowledge, skills, diversity of values, behaviours, and social and health structures in the delivery of patient care are overwhelming in the clinical environment. I acknowledge that student nurses in any country, including Malaysia, would admit to similar thoughts, feelings and experiences (Barnett, Namasivayam and Narudin, 2010; Birks, Chapman and Francis, 2009a; Egan and Jaye, 2009; Flanagan, 2009; Croxon and Maginnis, 2007; Higginson, 2006).

As with others who came from Malaysia, where activities of daily life involve integration and maintenance of cultural and traditional values and practices, a further adjustment was required on my part. Initially, a part of me resisted the differing values due to my desire to preserve my own cultural identity, so I attempted to use only purposive strategies to adjust to the ways of the new culture. Falsely, at that stage I believed it would help my survival through the theoretical and practice needs of my pre-registration nurse education. Quickly, I realised that everywhere I turned, I was confronted with my taken-for-granted and habitual ideas, values and behaviour. Only then did I realise that I could not remain as my former self and just use selective adjustment. The confusion, challenging attitudes, problems and experiences I was facing were eye-openers; an essential emotional, social and intellectual part of my intercultural learning experience. This is clearly in line with Anderson's (1994) view, that adjustment is related to short-term encounters, whilst adaptation is for long-term survival.

Over the next three years, the experience of living in the UK affected my attitudes, values and behaviour. Consciously I adapted to fit into the new culture by using my own resources and integrating new practices into my existing cultural ways (Dema and Moeller, 2012; Berry, 2005). I gained knowledge and confidence and understood words, social cues and patterns of communication within daily living, HE and nursing practice in the UK. Mainly, these were vital to succeed, to relate to patients and for professional relationships.

In the work setting, I observed other peoples' interactions and behavioural strategies (e.g. the use of touch and body posture) and cultural tools in their work (e.g. jargon) and gained understanding. Personally, I selectively let go of only certain of my socially learnt and established patterns and confronted some difficult issues. I enhanced my personal and cultural characteristics to find a sense of independence, responsibility, competence and personal strength, to perceive myself in a new and positive way.

This fits the stress-adaptation-growth model identified by Kim (2001) of people from different cultures who often are selective with the alternatives of being in a new environment. It assisted me to re-define and establish my priorities and my personal and professional identity. People learn from experience, anticipate, act with intent and then adjust accordingly as they go along (McHugh and Lake, 2010). Kramsch (2017) identified that even when one moves away from their community, one tends to retain previous ways of behaving and perceiving. This confirms that changes in beliefs and thinking take time and occur only when intercultural competences are acquired.

I stress that only with time, support and constant exposure, to alternative ways of knowing and doing, was I able to develop the skills to write in a different language. I also had to adjust, adapt and change my speaking, thinking and behaviour, through bad and good experiences, pleasures and pain, to reconstruct my cultural patterns to fit into a different cultural background.

In clinical settings, I felt more assertive and confident in myself to adjust to a less formal working environment and to accept the importance of best practice backed up with policies, procedures, professional standards and evidence. Being successful academically and professionally was mainly due to my compensating strategies related to motivation and effort. At the point of qualification, my identity as a nurse emerged because I was deemed to have developed the knowledge, critical thinking and reflection, understanding, competencies and skills required academically and in clinical practice to succeed professionally.

My experiences support Rudmin's (2009) view that intercultural adaptation and change requires support, sensitivity and guidance, over time, as the cultural shift demanded of international students cannot happen overnight. I found that western academics appeared to misinterpret the academic, health care, social and emotional differences. It led to inadequate teaching adjustments to support the learning needs of international students who, like me, had to make that transition to change. Thus, the degree of adjustment or adaptation made within the culture of the new environment depends on an individual's goals in life. I believe it also varies according to the needs of the situations, and/or type of environment that one encounters in a new culture.

Kim (1988) assumed that maintaining cultural ties and communication will interfere with the adaptation process, but I argue against it. Throughout my nurse education, I retained close ties with family and friends, even travelling back to Malaysia. This did not negatively affect my adaptation to the new culture, rather it motivated me to excel in my theoretical and practice assessments, to 'save face' of both my family and self. I argue that the original attributes that conflict with the cultural rules of the new environment remain dormant rather than become relinquished, as valuable resources are added to the original cultural rules.

This re-surfaces when one faces a similar situation or interaction, or when one returns to the former environment. Like many others, I quickly reverted to my old ways or cultural traditions when I returned to Malaysia, or even when I met a Malaysian settled in the UK. Sometimes, certain qualities are consciously replaced by new idealised cultural rules. It remains questionable whether one can truly leave their previous identity behind, but I believe some have abandoned their original culture in favour of an adopted culture.

Personally, I welcomed and appreciated many aspects of my changed identity, but, I have to admit that I regarded certain aspects, such as confronting and handling conflict, to be unintended side-effects of studying, living and working abroad and becoming part of a new community of practice (Wenger, 1998).

Influential professional stance

Professional stance describes the position one takes "toward knowledge and its relationships to practice" that occurs within social, historical, cultural and political contexts (Cochran-Smith and Lytle, 1999: 88). My professional stance integrated a reflexive account of my nurse and academic self to embrace the wider issues raised by both western and Malaysian societies.

As a Malaysian and UK nurse and academic

On completion of my nurse education, I worked in a variety of clinical areas. Initially, as a newly trained nurse, the focus was on providing direct patient care activities at the bedside. As I progressed in my career, my role moved away from the bedside to other care-related activities such as management duties, which led to changes in my thinking and attitude, and challenged my values and behaviour. Both the theoretical knowledge and clinical experience gained during my nurse education enabled me to provide care and teaching in line with UK values, HE and the health care system. Prior to my transition to academia, I became involved in aspects of teaching in clinical settings to enable other health professionals to update and maintain their CPD (NMC, 2011). My UK experiences enabled me to facilitate others to prioritise and organise nursing activities for safe patient care in clinical settings. Even with my adaptation to the UK culture, I needed to be mindful in every aspect of my work in order to avoid unconscious use of my former habitual and entrenched values and practices. Having lived my nursing life only in the UK, this connection directed my career and informed my own research.

In comparison, for nurses in TNHE programmes, their teaching and learning experience for each module with the western culture is only for a short one- or two- week period every semester over two years. Habitual ways of thinking, speaking, expectations and behaving may be challenged during the teaching period but, due to their short-term nature, the tendency to only make minimal adjustments is high. This is because the students eventually return to clinical settings where they are faced with others with ingrained cultural and traditional ways. Again, as the focus is on completing the assessments, there is a tendency that nurses may only adjust their thinking, writing and speaking in order to meet the assessment criteria to obtain the degree.

The option to implement change in clinical practice depends on the individual, as no practice component is attached to their TNHE programme of study. I argue that, intercultural adaptation is important to empower nurses to apply taught knowledge in clinical practice for improved provision of patient care in Malaysia. I refer the reader to the point I raised in my rationale, that the theoretical knowledge taught in the UK nursing programmes is in line with UK clinical practice, professional values and behaviour but conflicts with Malaysian nurses' cultural and traditional practices.

The national priorities of nurse education in UK universities since the Dearing Report (1997) recognised the contribution of HE to a skilled workforce. In nursing, this ethos provides the link between the theories taught in classrooms to enable nurses to carry out their role, and to understand what they are doing and why, and applying them within the boundaries of the workplace.

Previously, I acknowledged that the theoretical knowledge taught in HE enabled me as a student nurse to rationalise, learn or identify practices. This was because I was able to observe how other health professionals were delivering patient care within the workplace in either UK hospitals and/or community settings. Now, in academia, again I became aware that students who did not have the opportunity for practical experience, for various reasons, found it hard to apply the taught theory when they eventually went into practice settings.

Working within nursing and the educational field, I realised that my previous perceptions of nurse education as a Malaysian were important. I had to be sensitive towards using the eastern model as described by Cohen and Gunz (2002) within the openness and learner-centred approach of UK education. I also had to learn to re-define my teacher-student relationship from the previously acceptable way. I stress that the gradual broadening of my knowledge, skills, and confidence over time enabled me to adapt to teach within the western learner-centred system.

Influential researcher stance

To clarify the motivation in using hermeneutic phenomenology informed by an ethnographic principle of cultural interpretation, researchers often position themselves as either insiders or outsiders within their research domain. Both Merton's (1972) insider-outsider doctrine and Olson's (1977:171) two "mutually exclusive perspective frames of reference" circle around the researcher's relationship with participants. To determine either the in or out status, a combination of different dimensions must intersect. These dimensions include certain features of the researcher's identity (gender and ethnicity that are innate and unchanging), other features (age) that are innate but evolving, plus time, place and topic of the research, personality and power relationships between the researcher and researched (Perley, 2011). Neither position is privileged to see the "real truth as social experience and perception are continuously created by the social actors" (Cerroni-Long, 1994: 135).

Also, Merton (1972) defines the insider stance as based on the researcher's claim to the hidden knowledge of the community, to enable privileged access to the participants. The outsider stance is described as one who experiences the setting under study as a visitor and creates a picture of the setting for readers by being objective. In a social group, argues Burns and Grove (2008), not all may share similar perceptions, so they cannot easily be categorised, nor is the researchers' relationship with the researched static.

In reality, the differences are not clear. Both positions have advantages and disadvantages. Both reveal participants' reality, neither are purely achieved nor ascribed as the lines of separation are not distinct, so it is hard to tell where emic starts or etic stops. In the next section, the hidden values and dilemmas of my emic and etic positions from my personal cross-over and mixing between Malaysia and the UK is utilised. It informs and shapes the text of the process and experiences I faced throughout my research journey.

Malaysian and UK researcher as learner

The 'researcher as learner' stance identifies my struggle throughout the research process due to my lack of confidence in what I was doing. Firstly, despite this study being of great personal interest, after reading the literature I felt for a long time that I was in a maze. I kept venturing in different directions, returning to my starting point on numerous occasions, only to then head off in another direction. I was able to explain my thoughts regarding my research to others with clarity. However, to write and convey ideas and feelings in a precise manner in English at this level was fraught with difficulty. Eventually, I acknowledged that none of my previous study experiences had challenged my reading, thinking or writing with such focus and depth. As I started to develop my interview guide, my thinking started to align with my writing.

Initially, I had many pre-conceived assumptions, confirming Skeggs' (2002: 348) view that in all research, "the self of the researcher always or already exists". I also could not exclude my own voice. I repeatedly referred and compared the data with my experiences - as an international student nurse, UK nurse, academic and practitioner-researcher for cross-validation.

Malaysian and UK researcher within Malaysian culture

In Malaysia, the prerequisite for being an insider is being a Malay (main ethnic group). A Malay is defined as meaning "a person who professes the Muslim religion (Islam), habitually speaks Malay, conforms to Malay custom and is born and/or domiciles in Malaysia" (Constitution of Malaysia, Article 160, 1957). However, there are variations between the historical and socio-cultural factors. Despite differences between the constitution and socio-cultural definition, both are considered together (Ali, 2008).

An 'outsider' is someone who does not meet the requirements of being a Malay. All other ethnic groups, including myself as a Tamil Malaysian, do not meet the conditions of the Malay definition. I was born in Malaysia and had only ever known it as my home until I came to the UK. My position, like many other non-Malays, is strange. We have a dual stance; an 'insider' by being a Malaysian and an 'outsider' as a non-Malay. Despite not fitting the constitutional and socio-cultural definitions, in the reality of daily life and living, we are considered and treated as Malaysians. My study involved nurses from all ethnic groups, so it was vital to locate myself within the Malaysian tradition. It is not as a single 'us versus them' dichotomy, as implied by the official definition of being Malay. In this study, I intend to research my previous social identity group. They had similar earlier life experiences to mine, from before I came to the UK.

Having often travelled home, I had seen extensive developments taking place throughout Malaysia in an attempt to improve the status and progress of the country. Despite this, upon my return to Malaysia to conduct my study as a practitioner-researcher, I saw myself negotiating the hidden dilemmas of entry that my previous background had 'sensitised' me to. Schutz, (1976: 104) identifies "every social group... has its own private code, understandable only by those who have participated in it". But, I was conscious of a personal distancing taking place about the "strange and ... intriguing behavioural patterns and thought processes" of the people there (Ohnuki-Tierney, 1984: 584). I was confident that this unintentional stepping back would enable me to use my experiences selectively. It would minimise bias and provide objectivity, clarity and new insight that van Manen (2014) referred to as 'hermeneutic alertness'.

Some of my personal, professional and cultural values as a Malaysian were very deep-rooted. I was unaware of being insufficiently detached from certain values and they influenced me unconsciously. These taken-for-granted beliefs were challenged by my supervisors, or became evident in my reflexive journal. It was a revelation as I had assumed, I had adapted well to fit in with the western culture.

A Defining Moment

Malaysian and UK researcher collecting data in Malaysia

When I planned to undertake this study, I was aware of my dual stance within Malaysian society. Prior to returning to Malaysia for data collection, I also realised that my UK practitioner-researcher role was perceived to exude power, status and a threat. It meant I may be considered more as an outsider than as insider. Thus, I was unable to short-cut the mutual familiarisation phase, as personal relationships are vital to Malaysians.

To create a positive impression, I proceeded to arrange to meet the nurses (some opted to forego this meeting due to restrictions on time due to changes in working hours for the fasting month, or personal or family commitments). Their reactions to being researched were mixed - fear, pride and curiosity. I used an interactive format to instil trust and maximise exchange. On reflection, irrespective of whether nurses met with me or not, initially, all appeared self-conscious and displayed an appropriate 'front' (Goffman, 1959) by answering my questions with limited words, as depicted next.

> It is obvious they felt intimidated to say anything to me against the programme. They were in fear it may (even after receiving their results) affect them receiving their awards. They appeared tense and started off by checking if the interview was going to be in Malay. When I started the interview, the classic Malaysian 'smile and silence' attitude was very obvious. I felt frustrated!! Slowly as I started to speak in Bahasa Malaysia, used colloquial words and Malaysian humour, told them a bit about my own experiences as an international student nurse in UK and not forgetting, forthrightly telling them I was not evaluating the TNHE programmes or lecturers, they suddenly opened up. Information was revealed without me having to ask the question! As the interview progressed, I suddenly realised that I was speaking in Bahasa Malaysia whilst some were speaking in English and some even asked my professional opinion about certain situations.
>
> (Analytical notes, August 23, 2010).

I was confident that with, my being a Malaysian, the face-to-face interviews would enable rapport, due to my extensive knowledge, shared past history, ability to blend by observing the culture and conventions. Further, it would allow me to observe, recognise and interpret the unspoken but implied non-verbal cues that would enable me to probe further. The above analytical account confirms that, the strength of my interviewing lay in my ability to become part of the Malaysian social setting.

I considered myself privileged to interview these nurses, and admit that at times during an interview, when certain issues were being discussed, nurses appeared to view me as a temporary insider, or partial insider, due to my cultural identity. It appeared to relax them after a few minutes into the interview. It was also obvious that I had slipped effortlessly and unconsciously into a Malaysian insider role that connected with my biography, as I used colloquial words and humour when I observed any reservations. The advantage of being an insider was evident, irrespective of the Malaysian government's definition (Ali, 2008). Shared experiences led to interaction between myself and the nurses. It is impossible to tell whether it showed mutual commonality, but my friendliness, appeared to encourage candour and laughter as shared below.

> Whilst interviewee 016 was talking about others' acceptance to changes, she mentioned some staff will follow what she tells them to do, whilst others 'will make noise'. She continued, as a unit manager I would call them into my office; ask what the problem was for not following my instructions. Hmm...and they will come up with a thousand excuses, "macam-macam" [translated different types] excuses, some not even related with work ... We both started to laugh at the same time. It appeared to encourage her to further demonstrate her feelings through her facial expressions, the way she expressed and emphasised certain words and by what she said. She laughingly continued, 'I tell staff before you open [clinical area] door make sure your personal problems, you leave outside door, when going back collect it and go home'!
>
> (Interview data and personal notes: 25th August 2010).

My position shifted towards an insider in line with Patton's (2014) belief that the willingness to talk, and what is said, is influenced by who participants think the researcher is. At other times I was made to feel an outsider, due to my adaptation into the western culture. Nurses appeared to withhold information, perhaps as a defence or being careful not to comment on issues that may have negative repercussions (Gagliardi and Mazor, 2007), as my account reveals.

> She kept saying that what she learnt was fun and useful. I got the feeling that she appeared to be saying what she felt I wanted to hear rather than what she really felt or maybe to avoid offending me. Finally, 45 minutes into the interview she admits that 'not really anything I learnt I applied. The lecturers focus on, useful for assignment what we learn but can't apply in practice'.
>
> (Reflexive notes: 25th August 2010).

Participants may still align their responses to insiders in other ways, for other reasons, warned Patton (2014), as evidenced below where a nurse was hesitant to share her behaviour for fear of being judged by me. As an insider with insights based on shared lived experience, I was able to cut across ethnic lines and encourage her to voice her views, enabling "focus not on my own knowledge … but on the students' knowledge" (Belenky, Clinchy, Goldberger, Tarule, 1986: 218). Initial reserved responses were replaced with more confidential and detailed accounts. This contradicts Cerroni-Long's (1994) view that there are no benefits to being an insider. Understanding group dynamics is not based on 'in' or 'out' status but on the researcher's views.

> I will call them, of course you will get angry and say 'always late coming to work …, but … laughed, blushed and appeared embarrassed and was reluctant to continue. I encouraged her and after a few minutes she continued. You need to tone down actually, for example I sometimes hem … many, many times will tell, without you knowing it, right in front of everybody, so you actually aiming for

> and she pointed to her jugular vein she laughed and again appeared embarrassed and very hesitant to demonstrate her weakness so she stopped. I encouraged her to continue.
>
> She then said sometimes you are actually bogged down with many, many things. You are abrupt... sarcastic. Sometimes you cannot control, we human, we have our own problem, families, stresses, and dealing with young student, they are very restless, you tend to be very abrupt, but deep inside I know this is not right...
>
> (Interview and personal notes: 21st August, 2010).

Clearly, due to the sensitivity of the question under investigation, they said things I believe they would not have said to a non-Malaysian. They informed me they were telling me things in strictest confidence, and said 'you tahu lah' translated as 'you know lah what I mean', confirming they considered me as the person in the know!

Further, it was unlikely that the nurses would have voiced their views to a detached outsider, who, Schutz (1976) stated, had not been socialised into the group. Specifically, as in my study, to a westerner who is regarded to have a higher status than theirs. I also stress that as outsiders would not have engaged in the experiences that make up the life of these nurses, they would not have had the innate sensitivity that enables empathic understanding (Merton, 1972). I accept that the nurses may have provided more detailed information to a Malaysian within their own ethnic group or similar hierarchy level. It is noted that the insider's positioning and the establishment of trust for disclosure are hidden dilemmas decided only by participants (Beoku-Betts, 2004; Etherington, 2004).

Often, when I heard Malaysian nurses' responses, similar to that identified in the reflective account below, I was careful not to show any sign of surprise or agreement. On occasion, nurses' views were self-contradictory, as what they said at the outset was in conflict with their views expressed after a few minutes into the interview. Again, I remained as neutral as I could. This was the result of my past experience with the small-scale study I undertook in the first year of my EdD when my thoughts were revealed in my body language during the interaction and influenced the findings.

> I was careful when listening to her, making sure my facial expression and body language remained neutral. Sometimes I was tempted to shout 'yes! I was so excited at what she was telling me as issues I had faced as an international student nurse were being highlighted or issues that I had looked at in my rationale for undertaking the study were identified.
>
> (Reflective Note: 14th September, 2010).

To increase the validity of interviews, Polit and Beck (2010) warn researchers to have an open mind and not influence events in order to avoid misinterpretation. To enable this, Creswell (2011) suggests that researchers should first recognise, and then suspend, their cultural assumptions to see and understand another's. Initially, in my research journey, I fell into the insider/outsider dilemma with regards to my loyalty to both the TNHE universities and my interviewees, often taking on the role of sub-cultural spokesperson (Blackman and Kempson, 2016).

Hammersley (2012) argued that there is no middle way in research; the researcher is either committed to serving the interests of one group (TNHE University) or committed to serving the interests of the other (Malaysian nurses). I argue, over the course of undertaking the research, I developed the ability to became detached so as to embrace the views of the Malaysian nurses rather than my own personal experiences, or form an attachment to the TNHE universities, nursing profession, academics or the nurses. This was because my aim was to portray the voice of the participants accurately in the research text. I remained mindful not to allow my views to misconstrue what I heard nor to rule out other possible data and interpretations that arose. It reduced subjectivity, insider bias and unreliability and enabled me to undertake an intellectual discussion and avoid a "detour of my own or other's making" (Wolcott, 1999:348). My stance shifted with me looking from the outside in, and from the inside out, to understand both.

I sometimes noticed that, without thinking, I presented a professional front to the nurses in both my appearance and manner (Goffman, 1959), mainly to allow them to have confidence in me and my research. By creating my front, I used the same professional mask I would use in my work with other academics and students in the UK. Thus, my words and actions carried powerful meanings that appeared to maintain a Western approach. These are examples of how certain Malaysian cultural values and UK professional outlooks were imposed on the study, although they were mostly intertwined and somewhere in between.

When I was transcribing the interviews from the audio recordings, I became aware of the audibility of my voice and the clarity of my speech in Bahasa Malaysia. I realised that, as a multilingual Malaysian, I have always lived my life across languages and code switching was part of the way I have always communicated. Interaction across languages involves a transfer of facts, ideas, concepts and position to ascertain cultural meaning (Miola and Ramat (2015). Following transcription of the interview conversations, I translated the bilingual Bahasa Malaysia and English interviews into English. According to Temple and Young (2004: 167), "translation itself has power to reinforce cross-cultural relationships but that power tends to rest in how translation is executed and integrated into the research design and not just in the act of translation per se".

Through writing in the first person, I was able to use my multiple voices to write, re-write and reflect to situate myself in relation to the data I collected to understand and portray the voice of participants accurately in the text.

Chapter 4. Unfolding Malaysian nurses' views

The unique voices of the eighteen nurses from the demographic survey questionnaire and interviews are presented in this chapter. Interview extracts are shown in italics and are left in their original state, or as close to their authentic state as possible for those that needed translation into English. For clarity, where both Bahasa Malaysia and English were used in an interview, only the Bahasa Malaysia part of the conversation has been translated; so, despite the fluency of the speakers during the interviews, some extracts will appear disjointed. Slight discrepancies may also be evident due to the different use of idioms. Further, some quotes were edited to maintain the anonymity of the nurses and TNHE universities involved. An emic and etic outlook is articulated by means of cultural interpretation of the nurses' views to illustrate the meanings, values and behaviour to provide clarity for cross-cultural comparison.

Demographic characteristics

All eighteen participants were female, working in private hospitals and aged between 21 - 50 years. Two thirds of the interviewees were between 31- 40 years (12/18). No interviewee was aged over 50 years, maybe because in Malaysia nurses retire at the age of 56. Most nurses (17/18) had five or more years' experience and held senior positions. There were no restrictions on the number of choices nurses could select from the survey for their reasons for attending the TNHE programme. In the pre-determined answers, an 'Other' option was included to allow nurses to specify their reasons. The main reasons cited for seeking to upgrade themselves were: interest (14/18) and career development (12/18). Under 'Other', the reasons were 'self-satisfaction', and 'encouragement by father'.

TNHE post-registration top-up degree programmes

In the face-to-face interviews, reasons given for studying on TNHE programmes were like Interviewee **013**: *"My ambition to do degree"* and Interviewee **012**: *"standard isn't it western degree."* Still others thought the western degree was prestigious, as suggested by Interviewee **010**: *"UK, I always find higher quality."* None of them mentioned their entitlement to a graduate allowance in their responses to the demographic survey questionnaire but all, like Interviewee **018**, verbalised: *"I want RM$400 monthly allowance"*. These features were disclosed as an incentive.

The interview data confirms the assumption of status accorded to western education (Mok and Yu, 2013), and Hofstede's (1984) findings on long-term orientation in relation to work, where long-term rewards are expected. However, it conflicts with Chong, Sellick, Francis, Abdullah's (2011) findings where Malaysian nurses' main motivation to participate in local top-up degree programmes was to update knowledge and improve their skills, to raise their professional status and provision of patient care.

Six of the eighteen nurses interviewed self-funded their studies with a TNHE university with MQA accreditation approval. Their preference was not to have a contract with their employer, which would have entailed working for them for double the time taken to study. Priority for these nurses was to seek employment or career progression immediately after completing their degree, away from their current jobs and employers. Their lack of entitlement to any employment-based benefits led them purposefully to select TNHE universities that required attendance for a short teaching time-frame (to ensure only a minimum use of their days off or annual leave). They chose universities that offered theoretical knowledge only, with no clinical practice component. Other factors considered were low fees, no written exams and choosing an HEI with a good reputation offering modules like those offered by other HEIs.

In comparison, where TNHE programmes were offered by employers, they determined the type of programmes they were offering their nurses, i.e. twelve in this study. It appears that in choosing the programmes, MHE, MNB and employers failed to recognise the pertinence of a practice component run in parallel with TNHE theory. Employers' programmes also did not require MQA approval. Again, neither the MHE, MNB nor employers appeared concerned with this. Nurses disclosed that employers chose these programmes due to the perceived value of an overseas degree and the opportunity for all their nurses to obtain such a degree. On the other hand, nurses chose these programmes because of the paid tuition fees, extra study leave and the offer of free accommodation close to the study site during the teaching time-frame. Six nurses enjoyed the additional benefits of English Language tutors to enable them to obtain the IELTS qualification, and the support of a local co-ordinator during their programme of study.

This raises four issues in relation to my research. Firstly, as theory and practice is considered inseparable in nursing, the knowledge gained from reading, questioning and critical reading may have inspired evidence-based practice in clinical settings. This is evidenced by the literature which highlights that, as professionals acquire knowledge, they learn to problem-solve in routine or adaptive ways and move towards skill-based expertise (Brown, 2014; Cotterill-Walker, 2012; Mylopoulos and Regehr, 2011). It underlines the reasons Birks, Chapman and Francis (2009b), Egan and Jaye (2009) and Flanagan (2009) stress that taught theory must be relevant to clinical settings. It also supports Van Bogaert, Timmermans, Weeks, van Heusden, Wouters and Franck (2014), Rosa and Santos (2013) and Bellfield and Gessner's (2010) view of the importance of the theory-practice connection for enhancing the provision of patient care.

Next, the internal and external influences over the nurses' choices to study in TNHE programmes would have direct implications on their ability, motivation and decisions to apply theory in practice. Thirdly, when taught theory is combined with clinical settings, any resistance or challenges the nurses may have faced would have benefited from guidance, advice and support from TNHE academics. Finally, it aligns with the literature that suggests the difficulty of integrating classroom knowledge in clinical settings (Karstadt, 2011; Schober, 2013; Chong, 2013; Chiu, 2006; Birks, 2005; Hardwick and Jordan, 2002).

Intercultural teaching and the TNHE learning environment

Accent, language, teaching and learning styles

The participants were initially not deterred by the anticipated differences between eastern and western traditions. Instead, all indicated that they were mainly feeling positive despite mixed feelings of anxiety, fear and lack of confidence in their English Language skills and knowledge of western academic practices.

Fourteen participants highlighted their difficulty in understanding a pronounced accent from the UK and/or Australia. Interviewee **016** related her Australian TNHE experience:

> *"I found it difficult to the language, I trying to figure one word, she has finished sentence. She said one die [accent], I thought Oh dear! Who has died? Then I realise she actually meant one day!"*

Two nurses embraced the variations in accent and expression whilst another two did not find difficulty as they had previously worked in different countries with westerners.

All participants acknowledged the difficulty of coping with English as the medium of instruction. Even though nurses were familiar with English, it was not their first language but for some a second or third language. Interviewee **009** stated: *"At Malaysia we not speaking English only, we mix everything, all mixed language ..."*

Their spoken English freely incorporated a mix of words, or code-switching, from the languages of diverse ethnic groups' mother tongues (Yamat, Mustapa Umar and Mahmood, 2014). A coping strategy utilised is exemplified here: *"During class, all of us have the dictionary beside, ...*" (**Int: 011**). As a previous international student nurse, my etic view is that the pronunciation and enunciation of similar words and the slang used in the spoken English of western academics made it appear like a whole new language. Also, certain expressions used in casual speech are not found in dictionaries.

The western academics with their fluent English, subject knowledge, critical thinking and talking to learn approach, questioned nurses on their silent classroom behaviour: *"You all very quiet, never ask anything. ... We understand or don't understand we keep quiet only"* (**Int: 006**).

A combination of reasons contributed to their behaviour: a) deference to authority: *"We cannot be open, we have our national style, hierarchy, very, very obvious!"* (**Int: 013**); b) culture of listening to learn or to save face of the teacher: *"We give respect, we don't criticise or argue or give opinions"* (**Int: 010**); c) potential for repercussions: *"We have to accept, if we argue, they will say 'You are a bad student'. Then they will aim you and cut your marks"* (**Int: 006**); d) miscommunication: *"... when we ask question they explaining but we cannot catch what they are telling. Lastly, we give up"* (**Int: 002**); e) lack of comprehension: *"If we don't understand anything we don't know what to ask, right"* (**Int: 017**); and f) student saving face: *"If we ask then lecturer and others will think 'she is stupid lah to ask this question!' You don't want everyone to think you stupid so you keep quiet"* (**Int: 006**).

A key impediment that nurses identified in connecting with the academics was their feelings of inequality. Past colonial influence and their idealised merits of western education, so deep-rooted in their minds, affected them in line with Welikala (2013), Giroux (2010) and Ahmed's (2000) views. Interviewee **004** expressed *"We have English person coming to teach, we feel inferiority complex."* Questioning to make sense or justify knowledge was done privately or mentally which is evidenced by Interviewee **006**'s statement:

> *"She spoke about Indian patients in UK, but our nation, we used to Malays wear Malay clothes, Chinese, Cheong Sam and Indians, sari, they wear their traditional clothes. The lecturer*

said, 'Oh! No, let them wear their own traditional clothes'. I thought 'Why the big fuss about their clothing'? In Malaysia, we have already done it."

Even when they recognised that the academic was totally unaware of the cultural rules of Malaysians - for example, as she was telling them about practices that were normal in their daily lives, but which the academic thought was new information - the cohort responded as per Malaysian etiquette. They kept quiet to save face of the academic, as Interviewee **006** explained: *"Oh, never mind lah, she's a UK lecturer. ... she doesn't know or understand our culture, her culture is different. We have to accept her cultural diversity."*

Interviewee **004** described the acceptable way of interacting within communities and its direct influence behind their classroom behaviour:

"We're brought up to abide, listen to higher ranking. Indirectly, by showing respect, we cannot be extrovert, we become 'timid as a mouse'. UK, they teach to be outspoken that's why they are more forward compared to us. We will think first whether we gonna hurt your feelings and pull ourselves backward. This has been ingrained in us, this is in our blood."

The literature identifies differences between Malaysian and western learners in the classroom and typifies Malaysian learners as passive versus active (Biggs, 2014; Li, 2012; Chuang, 2012; Ales, 2010; Saha and Dworkin, 2009; Jedin and Saad, 2006). The difference in beliefs about learning also affects how they view the world, themselves and others. Fourteen of the eighteen nurses had previously experienced the didactic teaching mode that encouraged a silent learning style. My Malaysian emic view clarifies that students apply respectful listening and attention when the teacher speaks.

Chuang (2012) and Ales (2010) stress that certain hidden aspects of one's culture encourage or discourage classroom behaviour. In the TNHE classroom it created difficulties. Thus, it is important that the 'flying faculty' should have recognised these cultural rules as they influenced the nurses' expectations of the TNHE learning and teaching. From my UK academic stance, I highlight that these nurses were expecting the TNHE academics to give them all the relevant subject information necessary to elicit a correct answer for their assessments, rather than to verbalise their thought processes and develop enquiry skills that are key to independent learning.

There is an accepted assumption and a sense of security among Malaysians that not being active in the classroom does not mean lack of academic ability. Likewise, participating does not indicate academic prowess. Sayadi (2007) identified five inter-related factors that influence students' classroom participation: pedagogical, linguistic, cognitive, affective, and socio-cultural. The nurses' focused on knowledge as their main goal of learning and were behaving exactly as they would in a Malaysian classroom. Their polite, silent behaviour (Latif, 2017; Bryant, 2017; Mustapha and Nik Abdul Rahman, 2011; Abdullah, 2010) is attributable to their acceptance of power distance (Hofstede, 1984). In addition, Prime Minister Datuk Seri Najib Tun Razak in 2017 emphasised the need and acceptance to conceal negative emotions for social harmony. It reveals that interviewees' reluctance to participate was due to classroom etiquette as desired and defined by their home cultures, rather than their approach to learning or abilities.

Two TNHE universities, one UK and the other Australian, provided a mixed teaching and learning approach of face-to-face and distance learning. All nurses questioned the purpose of these intensive short contacts. They created confusion and feelings of being overwhelmed as they struggled with the accent, language, differences in nursing terminology and comprehension of the subject matter that were conflicting to them. Their inability to communicate with the 'flying faculty' was evident:

> "They teach us very fast. We will be like quite lost, because we will not have chance to [ask questions during] 9-4.30 or 5pm, they will be teaching only. When do we go and ask we don't understand this? They expecting us on the spot to ask, you know, we Malaysian we need time to go and personally to ask, you know. So we will be like keeping quiet only. When they finish, they say- ok, ok, see you all tomorrow. My lecturers all

> *staying in hotel so they will be rushing, the time 4.30 or 5pm, the driver will be waiting there, they will be rushing"* **(Int: 018)**.

My immediate insider opinion is that the time-frame described here conflicts with the slower approach and lifestyle preferred by Malaysians. In addition, the difference in beliefs about learning and support also affects how the nurses view others and themselves.

Twelve nurses had common views regarding the challenges of using other teaching and learning methods: *"Distance learning difficult especially if one is not IT savvy or have facility"* **(Int: 003)** and *" ... very tough lah because language problem"* **(Int: 007)**.

The lack of computer literacy was a significant issue in nurses' arguments against the notion of using online options. Learning to use technology, a key skill that most had to learn for the first time, prompted the question of whether such skills must be stated as a required criteria for being accepted onto the programme. For me, it clarified a possible reason for the poor response to emails I sent requesting participation in my study.

These participants expressed that teaching within the modules was very UK or Australia-centric rather than having an international focus. Interviewee **007** commented:

> *"I thought, why they don't give Malaysian examples, it's good we can know their ways but all from their practice. But here, we didn't see that, we don't know. Even if we know, we are not practicing, then how to relate. Especially when they give examples of equipment overseas, you know here we don't have and to get it is difficult, and the meaning is very different."*

All participants reported that it was obvious, apart from some Australian exceptions, that most TNHE academics had limited insight. Nurses assumed their knowledge was based on *"internet info, isn't it"* **(Int: 014)** and *"she Google lah"* **(Int: 013)**. This appeared to signify the lack of preparation of academics for their TNHE experience. Generally, nurses said: *"If they want to teach, they need to know our culture. Only then we can feel we can trust, easy to talk"* **(Int: 007)**.

The suggestion by Interviewee **007** above appears to be a desire to make transparent the culturally sensitive insights that are pertinent; this is because of their potential impact on learning and the application of theory in practice. It could be argued that the 'flying faculty' were operating based on their own academic models from which they were failing to acknowledge the above differences. Neither did they identify the extent to which these hidden differences affected nurses' learning. The findings confirmed Hofstede's (2001) view that in intercultural situations different values exist and these influence one's perception of conversations and behaviour. The data also confirmed Wu, Garza and Guzman (2015) and Ryan's (2011) summary of issues that may affect international students. It is also evident from the findings that, despite TNHE academics and Malaysian nurses having ways that may appear odd and amusing to each other as outside observers, the 'flying faculty' appear to have failed to cultivate intercultural "*savoirs*" (Byram, 1997: 148).

This raises the question of the need for educational preparation of academics prior to their teaching on TNHE programmes. Also, Australia's impressive amount of website information and literature on the importance of educational preparation for their academics (Lynch, 2013; Smith, 2009; Knight, 2008; Dunn and Wallace 2006; Leask, 2005; Crichton, Paige, Papademetre and Scarino, 2004, appears not to have made much difference.

Theoretical knowledge, assessments, and guidance and support

Participants were challenged by the subject-specific or specialised language and unfamiliar concepts in their modules. Additionally, the assessment criteria were difficult to decipher. The TNHE taught theory was assignment focused. After the teaching time-frame, participants expected face-to-face tutorials, follow-up guidance and support via email to complete their assignments.

Fourteen of the nurses were confused by the lack of clear-cut answers, or one standard version of an answer or a single correct method to complete their assessments, as was provided within their previous education culture. Nurses reported that they had developed their reasoning skills to rationalise the management of patient care. In Mylopoulos and Regehr (2011) study of nurses' judgement, the findings showed that, with experience, nurses developed a method of reasoning that enabled an intuitive understanding of the clinical situation in addition to their knowledge, skills, competency and experiences.

However, all felt challenged by the western critical analysis skills, to reflect on their knowledge in a cross referencing style and to re-evaluate information from the TNHE guidance. Also, to criticise others' work, to discern the value of evidence found, to be convinced or remain unconvinced by the evidence and to reason logically were difficult concepts to understand and master. This was because the notion of critical thinking and analysis is absent from the language and cultural frames of Malaysian society. Interviewee **018** stressed *"in our culture we don't really challenge, you know if authority says that's how you do it then that's how, what we do, there no debate."*

These participants could not make sense of this academic competency as they were not prepared for exploratory thinking that is both analytical and evaluative. They appeared to resent the short time span of teaching and the lack of sufficient academic support to enable them to develop, comprehend and achieve a good command of rational thought and decision-making skill. This is illustrated by the views of Interviewee **017**: *"I did nursing long time ago, our mentality is totally different, we need guidance. Capturing is not the issue but understanding is."*

My emic UK academic outlook recognises that Malaysian nurses' reasoning skills that are fundamental to management of patient care provision, reveal a distinction between how nurses reason in practice and the critical analytic skills required as an academic endeavour in TNHE programmes. Also, what TNHE academics considered as appropriate language, method and evidence to support critical thinking and analysis skills were western in nature and different from what these nurses were used to.

A few nurses expressed contradictory views. Interviewee **016** initially stated: *"Don't feel degree given me more knowledge, I can go to*

Internet. Wasted! Don't know right or wrong, we have to study ourself, so lack understanding."

Later in the interview she took a conflicting standpoint: *"Cannot use does not mean it is not good. One, we want to improve knowledge, even if cannot apply, at least you have knowledge and can check."*

Finally, at the end of her interview she appeared to clarify her own thoughts and concluded: *"Extra, extra [knowledge] to make change. If you go for a degree you need to learn more, not one or two things but substantial."*

In these programmes, the assessments were mainly assignment based. Thus, the criteria for successful completion were given on the first day of the teaching period:

> *"Time was short, actually at that time I wanted teaching to finish quickly, I didn't want to be with the lecturers because I didn't understand. I wanted to go back and finish my assignment. My focus is my assignment only, I didn't care about anything else"* **(Int: 008)**.

Clearly, learning behaviour and outcomes are related to the type of assessment. On reflection, my Malaysian notion is that learning by memorisation shows mastery of the knowledge gained from the teacher and textbook to pass examinations. Western assessments require nurses to seek information from a variety of sources, to then debate and justify by using academic writing conventions. The nurses felt they received limited guidance and support with this process, apart from broad explanations in the classroom.

The face-to-face teaching or distance learning period was followed by email contact with the academics for any queries about their assessments, which were then submitted on-line. Only Interviewee **004** reported support that enhanced her experience: *"I am very satisfied with some of the lecturers who are following you closely"*. Others reported inappropriate and/or insufficient support:

> *"Through email we can ask but how much can we ask, right. Even when we ask you see there is another cultural and language barrier. The way we ask they don't understand what*

exactly we want and they will be understanding different thing and they will be replying different thing" **(Int: 017)**.

Interviewee **008** said: *"Here we really want someone, not to say spoon-feed but to guide us ..."* Interviewee **002** stressed the academics' western orientation was evident by their lack of insight into Malaysian ways of support and guidance:

> *"They don't understand our culture. When break, we go to see them, they tell us sorry we having break and when finish class, they gone. ... What we don't understand, when we email often, they don't like it, ... we become a nuisance. They tell us to wait for response, then email, but sometimes no response for weeks! We felt abandoned."*

Regarding TNHE academics' assumptions, Malaysian nurses suggest that:

> *"Their perception is, it is distance learning so we have to take all the effort and do. I can't be asking another third party to come and teach me, because I am doing it with you and I am paying you so it is your responsibility"* **(Int: 017)**.

Exploration of support or lack of support provided for classroom experiences and assessments highlighted several questions; namely, a) what did the Malaysian nurses consider to be support? b) how would they normally seek academic support? c) why did most participants feel they did not get reasonable support? and d) in what way did the type of support received by one nurse enhance her learning experience.

More detail about what these participants considered as support was revealed by Interviewee **018** as needing time to go and personally ask. Interviewee **002's** point above further illustrates the typical way these Malaysian nurses sought support, which was during the break and when they finished the lesson. Also, Interviewee **002's** and Interviewee **017's** views and experiences with email support above identify why they perceived there was poor support. Interviewee **004**'s opinion of support that enhanced her learning is also evident above.

The difference is, in western countries, outspoken confident students generally ask questions of academics during teaching. Only a few silent listeners approach the academics at the end of the session. These silent listeners are not necessarily all international students (Bista, 2011). Further, students in western countries are provided with one-to-one or small group tutorials for completion of their assessments or in preparation for their examinations.

These Malaysian nurses felt they were being perceived as a nuisance. The academics had informed them not to email them repeatedly but to wait for responses. Often these nurses did not get an immediate response, and they stated that sometimes their questions had been misunderstood because the academics' responses did not reflect their queries. Another complaint was that they had moved on with their assessment, which meant they constantly had questions unanswered. Their lack of subject knowledge, poor response from academics, lack of insight of their accent, language and questions, led to beliefs that there was a failure on the part of academics to support their learning needs.

Culture and learning shock with coping patterns

Participants described how initial excitement quickly gave way to a sense of shock and disorientation that led to feelings of anxiety, frustration, uncertainty and self-doubts. The TNHE experience proved more demanding than they had expected, compared to their previous class contact hours and pace of teaching delivery.

> "Wah, I nearly felt like giving up … I don't know anything. I thought why did I take this course? If I know this is a very difficult course, I shouldn't take. I kept thinking to myself, why, why, why?" **(Int: 006)**.

They were also challenged when their previous styles of learning, e.g. memorisation to pass exams, had been replaced by a diversity of teaching and learning styles:

> "On-line ... Ooo difficult, everything have to learn, ... face-to-face teaching, our time so packed and we have to do everything. Maybe that is their way [delivery of teaching via on-line and short time-frame for face to face teaching], but we here they have to teach more [give in-depth and explicit information with increased face-to-face delivery of teaching] only then we will understand" (**Int: 013**)

Their experience of each module was summed up by all the nurses as similar to using a *"remote control"* (**Int: 010**) - *"switch on, switch off"* (**Int: 011**). Interviewee **016** clarified this succinct portrayal of the TNHE teaching as *"talk, talk, talk, fast, fast, fast then bye-bye"*. The *"compressed"* (**Int: 012**) or *"toooooooooooo short"* (**Int: 017**) teaching time-frame resulted in *"everything was like a blur"* (**Int: 009**). *"You not given the time to study something* [short teaching time-frame for each module]*, discuss and openly understand what is taught, we have info* [information]*, its just info only"* (**Int: 017**).

Nurses' feelings were compounded as they perceived that the TNHE delivery took place against what they understood to be good learning and teaching practices, as too much subject knowledge was taught within an unrealistically short time-frame. They were deprived of a 'honeymoon period', which Oberg (1960) points out is necessary and provides time for a gradual adjustment and acclimatisation to the new thinking, writing and academic practices like those required for TNHE programmes. My data supports that initial transitional experience in any different cultural environment is a *"painful and testing process"* (Brown and Holloway, 2008: 243).

All eighteen nurses stated that the real problem began when the assessments and criteria were given, especially for the fourteen nurses for whom it was their first experience of writing assignments. Initial reactions included anxiety and uncertainty that they could rise to this challenge. These early doubts were followed quickly with questions of how to meet the criteria for assessments as explained:

> "You know our English standard here, speaking and writing how we will be writing our essays. 500 words also we will be struggling to write in English. In diploma we answering a,b,c,d

> *- that's what we learn; suddenly to do essay style 2500, 3000, 5000 words is quite hard. You know to make up a word, to make up a sentence, to make it longer, we find is very difficult"* ***(Int: 018).***

All participants attached importance to academic achievement. Thus, after their initial flight response, they quickly recognised the need to use coping strategies to fight and overcome their shock and confront the challenges. The tendency for international students to take flight or fight when confronted with obstacles was acknowledged by Anderson (1994).

Keeping a dictionary beside them in the classroom was a major coping mechanism that continued throughout their programme of study (18/18). They also talked to others in the cohort, family, colleagues, friends (18/18) and, if available, the local co-ordinator (6/18). It was evident the main purpose of talking was to come to terms with their emotions and gain advice and support, as consistent with research findings on coping with culture and learning shock (e.g. Teras, 2013; Boland, Sugahara, Opdecam, and Everaert, 2011; Ryan, 2011; Joy and Kolb, 2009). A third and parallel coping strategy was their seeking help from others or getting together in small groups with nurses in their cohort for discussions.

Selective adjustments and adaptations

Their own traditions of learning were incompatible with these new approaches. The idealised western qualification that these nurses deem superior pressurised them to adjust, thus motivating them selectively to explore, develop and change to new ways of learning for the instrumental end. They used Information Communication Technology (ICT) to gain access to the in-depth knowledge and planning required, questioning and thinking through principles and theories to add to their original repertoire (18/18). Their beliefs about effortful and respectful learning were valuable cultural resources. Participants resorted to and transferred these across learning cultures in dealing with adjustment demands. It remained the main coping strategy with their academic work.

The skills required for academic achievement are generally acquired over time, as identified with my emic view as a Malaysian. As nurses' previous learning focused on assimilation of information and providing correct answers, so they struggled with the new academic literacy skills. Further, these nurses had to fast track their learning to complete the assessments within the short period allocated for each module in the programme. Systematically working through the reading materials assisted some in completing their assessments. Others stated that the assignments given were the same with only slight changes every year, Interviewee **016** said:

> *"Some staff said, for us it is easy, we just take the senior's assignment and copy or cut and paste, change the sentence slightly. Some of us struggle to do the assignment! The way we are taught and assessments must change."*

Six nurses studying with one UK university were required to complete a dissertation for the Honours component of their programme. It was delivered via distance learning, so there was no face-to-face teaching or guidance. Also, there was unsatisfactory email contact from supervisors. They were angry!

> *"They didn't teach but expect us to do, they totally don't have idea. Very difficult, for a culture that hadn't written assignments, to do research project no support! Keep asking people around, who done Masters, lecturers who done PhD, like a nuisance going around asking. ... they question you, didn't they teach you? Not worth, RM$18000"* (**Int: 015**).

This interviewee's previous didactic teaching and learning experiences were still impacting on her new learning.

For others, like the six participants from the other UK university, their lack of understanding of the required criteria, assessments and the poor face-to-face, on-line and local co-ordinator support, led to their whole cohort having to re-submit their work. The drastic variance in academic writing style only became evident after submission of the first assignment. When the academic realised that none of the students had met the criteria, she arranged via their local co-ordinator to meet with them. They had stunned reactions when informed of their failure to meet western academic standards for their English language, the inadequacy of their study skills and critical evaluative thinking. This was verbalised by Interviewee **010**:

> *"Very hard, most of us doesn't know what we doing, we had to write 5000 words, it's not medical words but this is totally different. First module we all didn't meet criteria, so all had to do it again. Only then knew our English not good. She said be more critical, not descriptive – how? Reference list, key point in each paragraph and some other things and plagiarism taught on another extra three days. This was not told in the two week teaching period."*

The culture of simply memorising text rather than critiquing and rationalising affected how they completed their assignments:

> *"Guidelines given on database, but not useful. No, it is a struggle. I put in A-Z whatever I know or feel I want, just pour it in my paper, I have to open book, see what is in their content and then I copy in to my content"* (**Int: 003**).

Interviewees **006, 016, 002, 010 and 003** above highlight the implications of poor TNHE academic support. This will be addressed later in this chapter.

The reality of their TNHE experience was summed up by Interviewee **014** as she compared what it might be like for students in similar programmes in the UK:

> *"Tough! In UK they learn for a long period, three four months, but here in Malaysia it is for only two weeks, everything has to enter immediately. We are like blank, blank! Not enough [time to gain understanding of knowledge or discussion], difficult to cope, teach, teach, we want to ask questions no time."*

Overall, so far, there appeared a mismatch in expectations and pedagogical context between the western and eastern cultures. It caused anxiety, and nurses perceived it as a source of culture and learning shock (Davidson, 2013; Teras, 2013; Joy and Kolb, 2009;

Thomas, 2005). Further, the qualitative data confirms Widdowson's (1990) assertion that to communicate with an individual from another culture, there must be awareness, understanding and interpretation of cultural differences.

Eventually, it led to the nurses using coping strategies. This supports Kim's (2001) theory that communication is key to facilitating transition from one culture to another. It also supports her stress-adaptation-growth dynamic model of adapting only to meet essential conditions of the new learning system, whilst maintaining cultural rules. My opinion is that her theory is relevant to both nurses and the TNHE academics.

The above sections have critically reviewed participants' perceptions of their TNHE teaching and learning experiences. It also identified how they dealt with the demands of their study programme in the new academic context. Based on the data, it appears: a) classroom experiences were short, overwhelming, western centric and assessment focused; b) TNHE academics appeared unaware of the reasons for these nurses' classroom behaviours, their education and health care systems; c) among the taught modules, only certain theory had been of interest, understood and added value and depth to their existing knowledge and practice; d) preferred method of asking questions was face-to-face, in private or on a one-to-one basis after teaching; e) email contact needs to be enhanced; f) writing assignments was a new experience for most nurses, g) academic standards varied but too little explanation was given on how to meet them, and h) explicit assessment criteria was desired. Key issues are raised here regarding the influence of these factors on nurses' learning, motivation and their ability to transfer and apply the TNHE taught theory in practice.

Impact of TNHE theoretical knowledge in clinical practice

In relation to the research aim, it was essential to identify if and how nurses were making sense of the taught theory, in what ways it helped shape their identities and how they translated the knowledge across populations (western to eastern) to apply it into practice.

Personal development of nurses

A sense of personal achievement and recognition by others was evident with all these nurses as stated by Interviewee **011**: *"everyone respects you more because of degree"*. In addition, nurses who studied with the UK TNHE programmes admitted feeling a higher level of pride as theirs had an added title of Honours degree. Interviewee **006** said *"When I passed, I felt relieved, happy and proud. My son said Wah! Mother you also have a degree. I said yes, not just degree but UK Honours degree."* The six nurses from the Australian TNHE programme still valued their achievement: *"... proud I have degree, even if only degree"* (**Int: 016**).

Intellectual outcomes noticed were improved knowledge, English language proficiency, keenness to read and interest to question. There was enhanced insight to access and gather information, and improved academic writing skills. Attaining the degree was considered by fifteen nurses as an indicator of their intellectual ability, which boosted their self-confidence: *"I changed a lot, ... read more and more, more knowledgeable. So I am more confident. Before I went to work and came back, like a robot"* (**Int: 006**).

Their previous routine ways and practices that helped them maintain a sense of comfort and security were challenged and led to personal growth. This echoes Llopis's (2014) view that learning enables letting go of a past identity and perceiving the self in a new and positive way. The other three nurses felt they had always been self-confident, for example *"No change, I always confident"* (**Int: 016**).

Information Technology skills (IT) contributed to intellectual growth, enhanced their sense of achievement, improved self-confidence and autonomous ways of knowing. Using on-line learning, resources and support was considered extremely difficult by some nurses. In fact, those frustrating experiences had positive results for some in clinical settings, as evidenced by Interviewee **011**'s point:

> *"Interest to find out, certain terms I don't understand, I will go and search in the internet. Before, I just ignore or not my job or ok if I don't know that, as long as I can understand what I need to understand."*

Critical thinking was reported by a few nurses to have become part of their daily lives since their exposure to the questioning required for analytical thinking processes to meet the criteria for their assignments. Interviewee **017** explained: *"Even choosing my indoor plants for my new house, I question, gather all the evidences, I looked for the right plants not just simply buy any plants."*

The learning behaviour of Malaysian adult learners indicate an emphasis on short term and immediate motives such as career advancement or to save face rather than for an intrinsic valuing of lifelong learning (or extrinsic value of extra pay) as Tan and Pillay (2008) posit.

However, exposure to TNHE programmes, for all their nurse-reported shortcomings, did appear to have transformational effects on the nurses' relationships with aspects of learning. For one nurse, it increased academic options: *"I finish degree then started Masters"* (**Int: 001**). A few others related that it has given them the confidence to consider furthering their study (**Int: 002, Int: 003, Int: 005, Int: 008 and Int: 013**). This is counter to what Tan and Pillay (2008) stated. However, Tan and Pillay (2008) are right in that the motivating factors for all nurses were their personal achievement, recognition of status accorded to a western degree, the extrinsic financial reward and career advancement. There is some evidence here that the nurses' motivations had a more lasting impact on at least some of their learning behaviours.

The data indicates an overlap between personal achievement, enhanced intellect, development of information technology and critical thinking skills which led to improved confidence and personal growth as an outcome of the TNHE experience.

Professional transformation in nurses

For twelve nurses, the sponsorship of the programmes by their employers enabled them to achieve their personal aim and career promotion, or the potential of a promotion when a vacancy arose. The six nurses who self-funded were motivated by their future career prospects and employment mobility. Malaysian culture considers academic qualification to be synonymous with status: *"I was a senior* but was not recognised by management. When I finished my degree, only then I recognised" (**Int: 008**). This recognition for Interviewee **007** also draws attention to her previous self-perception in contrast to her newer self-image: "[In the past, I] *accept I am a nurse, just a nurse, not a professional.*"

Similarly, Interviewee **014** noted: "Before when I work, I follow what I learnt at my School of Nursing, that is what I follow, no name, just do. After doing degree, only then I know, name and why doing" (**Int: 014**). This personal and professional shift was further stressed by Interviewee **005**:"*Before I didn't think, no critical thinking, just do and do only, now I think.*" And yet again by Interviewee **009** who said:

"When management e.g. collect data, last time questionnaire, we so busy, we just tick, didn't even go through it! Now we learn, we understood, collect data to improve work, not give extra work, so we take time, read and do properly."

Recognition for change with regards to the doctor-nurse relationship was noted:

"We are timid, like a mouse with doctors, I think we should emulate western outspoken kind of attitude, little bit into our society and health care settings. Sometimes we need to tell off the doctors for the patient's sake" (**Int: 004**).

It can be seen so far that personal development was linking directly into enhancement of their professional interpersonal skills:

> "More sure of myself in problem solving, ... how to give orders, I'm more confident with my communication, diplomatic way. When I handle students and staff, I use sandwich technique, hopefully they learn something lah. In the past and now the same but the thing is now I polish up my way" (**Int: 004**).

Questioning, reasoning and their newly-learnt knowledge enabled some nurses to engage with nursing care decisions: "*Now, I feel more complete the way I nurse the patient, not just do and go. I take the initiative to spend time with the patient, ... find out their views or their needs*" (**Int: 011**).

Certain nurses developed the ability and confidence to test out new interests in their daily working life. Several developed positive professional attitudes towards their capabilities: *"Initially I don't like management post, don't like me be in charge, not on management. After course, ... why not try, give a try, now I manage unit"* (**Int: 002**).

The findings confirm Ng, Tuckett, Fox-Young, Kain (2014), Lillibridge and Fox's (2005) and Davey and Robinson (2002) study that most nurses who gained a degree attained increased self-confidence. The reality of transforming oneself versus altering others' attitudes towards change were agreed by all in the following terms: *"Change easier in me than being able to change others"* (**Int: 003**). This often has indirect benefits for patient outcomes; for example, nurses can interact more equally with other health professionals to enhance patient care.

Also, the qualitative data supports Darbyshire's (2006) and Des Jardin's (2001) view that as nurses acquire knowledge and skills, they become empowered. Opportunities to apply taught knowledge, when supported by their employers, were found. *"We have a journal club in hospital, who study research in degree, we meet and discuss"* (**Int: 014**) and *"I get involved and learning from others, now I trying to use my knowledge"* (**Int: 010**).

The question to which I now turn to is whether they applied the theoretical knowledge they had acquired through TNHE to improve the provision of patient care in clinical settings?

Implementation of theoretical knowledge in clinical practice

Interviewee **004**, together with Interviewee **015**, (they had studied with two different UK TNHE universities), sought to use their new theory about evidence based practice:

> *"We did observational studies, we go all around the wards ... we analyse, tabulate and present during meeting, our ... was impressed. And the results were circulated to all the unit managers. Having evidence from your place, we able to speak out and make comparison with WHO standards, they were like Wow!" (**Int: 004**).*

There were inconsistencies in viewpoints, throughout individual interviews, with regards to whether nurses had made changes in practice settings. For example Interviewee **015**'s account of changes she had implemented: *"nothing really can apply in practice"*. And this does support Silverman's (2000) warning of a gap that exists between beliefs and action. Yet this same interviewee talked about using her learning and confidence in strategic ways:

> *"... helped me a lot how I talk to Doctors in meetings. When I say it is the National Health Service UK evidences actually said ..., many of us like to use that to present to Doctors, because they don't ask any more questions! Back to culture and this perception that British are best. Because we colonised, their influence is still there and we look up to them, their very good reputation still remains. Immediately, Doctors say is there anything that we can adopt."*

Here is a clear disparity between opinions in relation to actions (Weber, 1947). Amongst other interviewees, acknowledgement of professional responsibility also led to reflection on previous practice:

> *"The importance of incident reporting e.g. infections or diseases. In the past we keep quiet"* (**Int: 009**) and *"sometimes we know it is important but we don't do e.g. to maintain documentation. We have to change our own way"* (**Int: 013**).

Clinically related modules prompted Interviewee **007** to consider reducing the risk of pressure sore development:

> *"I said, turn patient every hour or two hours, before every three or four hours. I explain why we do, our care must be quality. I tell them record on form when turn patient."*

What was evident was that most did not accept certain aspects of the *status quo* in which they had returned to work; they had the confidence to make changes to management of patient care. Areas to which nurses were now directing their attention included the clinical environment, handling and managing of other health professionals, student nurses and patients, and reporting of patient information and documentation.

The extent to which TNHE theoretical knowledge was being applied in clinical settings remains unclear and cannot be ascertained due to differing views and the limited number of examples given. This in turn indicates the difficulty of ascertaining where and how theory and practice were linked. In terms of scale, Interviewee **003** suggested: *"Implementation of change, on a smaller scale, yes, but in a big scope, no."*

Acceptance of nurse-led changes

Before I can discuss the acceptance of nurse-led changes, there is a need to review the status of nursing in Malaysia. I refer the reader to Chapter 2 above, where Bryant (2017) is cited as saying that in Malaysia, nursing is still considered a menial job. Interviewee **007** confirms this as she related her relative's comment:

> *"… do you need degree to clean faeces? You don't know, I really felt it. People look at nurses as the lowest, they only see we look after others, … faeces, vomit, … Despite degree, peoples' perception has not changed, still think dirty job, culture lah. They don't see nurses help them recover, they think its Doctors."*

Another nurse, Interviewee **001**, had a different viewpoint: *"Status perception has changed, in the sense of education level, even though performance not good. Most Malaysian nurses already done Masters, PhDs!"*

With regards to management, four nurses thought they would accept change if it benefitted patients and staff. Others, like Interviewee **016** argued: *"Management don't like if we develop … culture and politics. You talk no use, they don't listen."*

Questions emerged from this data of why employers buy into TNHE programmes for their nurses but resist changes for best practice that the nurses then offer them.

Attitudes of other health professionals affected their keenness and motivation:

> "… they saying it should be based on evidence but if culture does not support nurses verbalising and thinking out of box then it is not leading to patient safety. Here, there are nursing managers who have done degrees and yet their degree stays at home. The knowledge stays at home, it doesn't come to the workplace, they are still the same, as how they were. They happily walking about and not implementing anything. My leaders are different from the leaders from the book" **(Int: 015)**.

Most nurses had views similar to Interviewee **015** above, and my insider emic view supports the reasoning of Interviewee **002**:

> "Culture in Malaysia, they don't see change will give them any benefits, they only see reward. If I do this, what is my reward, they don't see the higher reward like job satisfaction."

Deference to authority was also demanded as Interviewee **006** was told: *"I'm the unit manager, I'm senior than you'. Then you cannot overrule her, our hierarchy level is different. … I felt frustrated."*

Hierarchy seemed to persist and was a difficult challenge for nurses to overcome, as overruling hierarchy was unacceptable:

> "We tried to go and meet the …, She said she can accept the change but you have to inform your unit manager. Your unit manager will have to complete the paperwork and give me" **(Int: 006)**.

Bryant (2017) asserted that the medical profession in Malaysia regards nursing more favourably than does the public. Nurses expressed the view that doctors who updated themselves and were trained overseas respected nurses and their opinions. This is confirmed by Bryant (2017). In comparison, those who followed traditional ways or who had been educated in Malaysia preferred to maintain the *status quo* as "… they still think they are God" **(Int: 012)**, and we like their "*handmaidens*" **(Int: 001)**.

Interviewee **007** points out: "Doctors look at nurses like stupid, you just follow what I say, like nurses no brain lah". She further voiced her frustrations as she summed up her reality: "Some doctor don't want this, don't want that, don't want this. Here Sister you do like this, you follow my style. Three Doctors three styles so ...".

All eighteen nurses believed their newly achieved graduate status had little impact upon acceptance of change by nurse colleagues. They found senior nurses, commonly known in Malaysia as *"hard core"* (**Int: 004**) with their *"rigid mind-sets"* (**Int: 001**), were more *"difficult and stubborn"* (**Int: 012**) towards accepting proposed changes. Reasons cited were satisfaction with their senior status, long service and complacency. Also, their confidence with the routines resulted in their preference to remain within their comfort zones. Interviewee **005** said: *"Even with their eyes closed they know what to do, to re-learn a new way of doing things, they don't like."*

Nightingale's (1859) comment that experience is not conducive to learning and Shiffrin and Schneider's (1977) experimental data support this. This is because habituated thinking and actions are unconscious and difficult to unlearn.

> Some junior nurses, too, opposed change, as Interviewee **003** said: *"They see as extra work or extra paperwork e.g. this year another new chart, to them is hell. They don't see importance of compliance. Their attitude, if I don't do so what?"*

Interviewee **003** reported that sometimes changes that were implemented in practice failed to continue:

> *"They take idea, initially accepted but not well implemented e.g. I doing a project, quality improvement benchmark with a lot of references, to use form for ... but staff don't record. It remain a form!"*

Similarly, Interviewee **007**, noted above as trying to make changes to patient turning to reduce the risk of pressure sore development, found that staff *"... didn't do, or not doing correctly, or do only when see me."* Again, professional transformation was clearly linking into shifts in personal communication styles. To encourage compliance for implementation of change, participants who held management positions reported that they used: *"diplomatic discussion, first; if don't listen then I say I manager, you have to follow"* (**Int: 005**).

It was known that nurses followed instructions out of deference to managers' authority, rather than their education and knowledge. Some senior nurses were said to be disinterested in furthering their studies, but were resentful of the degree holders' academic attainment. This is because it resulted in an immediate rise in status and salary, and changes that the new graduates introduced to their comfortable work practices. A senior nurse herself, Interviewee **006** dealt with resistance from anti-degree nurses as follows:

> *"We have to talk to them with respect, because they are senior but we have to be positive thinking. Another thing, they don't like when you say it is based on research. They will say 'Yes lah, you went for course, so you know lah, I didn't go for course. Their thinking is, I have learnt higher than them, better to just follow lah. We use gentle approach and they follow like they are forced."*

With regards to patients, all participants concurred that: *"… patients, whatever you want to do, they will agree"* (**Int: 009**). This is important as it indicates that patients generally trusted nurses with their care and had a positive approach to change, irrespective of whether that change was instigated by nurses who had a degree. The other aspects impacted on the theory-practice connections are identified below.

Outcomes of TNHE experiences and qualifications: nurses' evaluations

Participants' initial perceptions were that teachers and book knowledge were authoritative sources. Based on the findings, it seems that when they became aware of the value of being a critical reader and writer and using evidence for practice, they did not appreciate being taught only the theoretical knowledge. Interviewee **010** said: *"She didn't link research to practice, even if Management* *give chance, don't even know where to put it because didn't show me."*

Throughout the programme, these nurses were focused on attending the classes or undertaking on-line sessions to complete their assessments for achieving the degree. At a personal level, they did not give the application of TNHE knowledge in clinical practice any serious consideration. On completion of their degree, they became aware that the lack of a clinical practice component inhibited their ability to apply the learning in practice. Interviewee **001** said:

> *"I can't even remember [TNHE theoretical knowledge]. How we can remember? We learn and put into practical we can remember always. Is not related to our work, no ... cannot apply in practice!"*

The six nurses who self-funded all purposefully chose TNHE programmes with only a theoretical component. Post-course, they realised: *"Culture is different, difficult to understand. Understanding of theory is different when you can apply in practice. Must have practice, this is nursing not accounting"* (**Int: 014**).

Nurses in programmes provided by their employers argued:

> *"They didn't mention about practical so we kept quiet. We learn theory because you want to do something about your practice because there is a problem. If you don't know how to use the theory or cannot use in practice to settle the problem, why do you want to learn the theory"* (**Int: 005**).

Participants believed if a practice component were part of TNHE programmes, when facilitating change with the new perspectives, the 'flying faculty' guidance and support could be called upon during their clinical experiences. This would enable them to learn different strategies to overcome challenges they may have faced.

Another Interviewee **001,** who studied with the Australian TNHE programme, stated: *"... our employer take it not for quality, just* [accept] *for ranking and qualifications. To advertise all nurses' have* *degree."* Her view confirms that international partners may be selected to gain prestige and ranking by association (Williams, 2012).

Some nurses also stated they were disappointed by their academic achievement, as it did not accurately reflect their knowledge, understanding and ability to make the theory-practice connection. This is illustrated by Interviewee **017** who self-funded:

> *"If you ask me about [how to apply] research [at work], sorry I not able to tell you, even with doing research project, because my understanding is not good enough. So I feel embarrassed in that way. I even now thought of going for short research methodology courses in Malaysia. You have to pay quite a lot of money and you go like one week course but again what is the point of taking it from this TNHE university and now I have to pay again. It's a waste!"*

Certain nurses from the UK university, who were sponsored by their employer, were dissatisfied: *"We didn't do research project. I know, other UK university did research project for honours. Our honours degree like Australia, four modules only"* (**Int: 012**). These nurses appeared resentful that their learning did not reflect the knowledge required to achieve the Honours title. Instead they felt it was similar to a general degree rather than reflecting a higher level Honours degree. Hence, it was perceived to be of a lower status compared to the other UK university.

All participants accepted TNHE programmes in Malaysia, as Interviewee **013** stressed: *"provided an opportunity to obtain a degree"*, but some like Interviewee **008** stated: *"... want the degree to learn"* and stressed the need for quality programmes rather than those that were as Interviewee **017** said *"... two weeks, assignment based, I give you certificate degree and finish"*. Others, *"... just want the paperwork"*. Six nurses said that they were pleased when one UK academic, on their first day and whilst introducing the programme, said: *"don't worry end of the day you will get it, get a degree!"* (**Int: 002**). Interviewee **001** from another TNHE university stated:

> "Personally, I think everyone don't mind because they still get their degree and RM$400 allowance. Knowing and not knowing the depth of degree studies not important, so long as they got the rank and the qualification."

The consequence of a theory-practice gap was voiced by Interviewee **015**: *"Danger of learning theory but no practice – don't know how to adopt theory and blend into our culture or what you are doing, why we doing it, can put a patient at risk - safety"*. There was also reluctance to apply TNHE taught knowledge in clinical practice as they preferred to retain their original cultural values: Interviewee **007** said: *"I want to learn but want to keep my culture."* It confirms Wenger's (1998) belief that resistance within communities can be implicit, subtle and informal. It further highlights the importance of recognition by TNHE academics of culturally sensitive insights that Malaysian nurses have.

Interviewee **009** explained *"... we need to follow what patient say, we need to follow their culture. They from small have been taught, so that is their belief, then we have to follow, we cannot argue with them."* This comment reveals how far Malaysian culture and diversity affects nurses' professional practices which may have been poorly understood by the 'flying faculty' academics. These perceived cultural differences contributed to the *"theory-practice gap"* (**Int: 007**). All participants gave specific examples of ways of caring that differed between the eastern and western culture. Interviewee **013** said, *"Here we don't have hired translators in hospital. Family members will be the translators, they want to know everything. There is no privacy."* Another Interviewee **006** said:

> *"We studied the patient has rights, but in Malaysia, the rights are given to the children. When the Doctor asks for consent or anything, overseas they will say, 'I will think about it first' but here, 'wait until I speak to my children'."*

Relatives tend to make decisions on the patient's behalf which overrides the patient's autonomy and their right to know. Abdullah (2010) explains it is not just paternalism but deeply held beliefs surrounding individual choice and rights. Specifically, I ask the reader to consider the cultural connotations of the values.

> *Interviewee **006** stated, "When we are young our mother cares for us, we look to her for everything. Now our mother is old, she will look to the children for decisions," which Interviewee **012** expressed as "It's our way of bonding with our family, ... showing we care." Interviewee **005** added: "... it also protects our relative from the truth." With my emic perspective, I confirm this is one of the shared attitudes about families between all ethnic groups in Malaysia. Parents provide for their children in return for unconditional loyalty and obligation (Alavi, Sail, Idris, Samah and Omar (2011)).*

These examples identify how Malaysian nurses are required to integrate their practice in line with the WHO's and MNB's (2002) professional standards. In addition, they are required to provide care alongside the culture and traditions of the diverse ethnic groups.

Nurses outlined how the western professional standards appeared to override local cultural and religious practices. However, they were expected to integrate western professional standards alongside the Malaysian philosophy to fit the cultural context of the diverse ethnic groups within society. *"They don't know our way, they just come and teach their way and go back thinking we can do, but no, we can't"* (**Int: 010**).

Interviewee **002** further explained:

> *"We learn UK culture and in UK hospital it is UK culture. In Malaysia, they teach UK culture but difficult to blend UK culture in our health care, because patient, other staff and management must all want to change."*

The status of TNHE degrees and their impact afterwards in the nurses' clinical settings, irrespective of the theory-practice link, is illustrated by Interviewee **004**:

> *"Before this, we have been doing this for long, long time nothing happened. Since came back from UK course [sarcastic],*

they don't say 'with honours', they say 'with horns' [referring to shortened word for honours – hons.] so the horns have appeared [she demonstrated with her fingers to signify horns]."

The self-funding nurses' TNHE university had MQA accreditation whilst the employer-funded TNHEs did not have MQA accreditation. But nurses became aware of this fact only on completion of the programme. However, the TNHE degree award entitles all nurses to the financial incentive and the potential for promotion regardless of whether their programmes had been accredited by MQA. The long-term consequences of having a degree that did not have MQA accreditation would need to be seen. At present the employer-sponsored nurses are bonded or have a contract for four years. In contrast, the choices and prospects for promotion for the self-funded nurses are varied and extensive.

Issues arising from analysis of data

The extent to which the TNHE theoretical knowledge has been applied in Malaysian clinical practice has been determined from their views. The consensus among the eighteen nurses was that the culturally constructed status and role of nursing, hierarchy, financial resources and time implications failed to offer the opportunity or support for applying learning in clinical settings. Difficulty in changing the resentment, attitudes and performance of nurses who were recruited without a degree and preferred not to study further was a source of frustration. But, these nurses were optimistic that with the increase in the number of degree nurses, there will, in time, be less resistance and increased motivation to apply TNHE learning in practice. Their belief supports Hardwick and Jordan's (2002: 530) view that *"a workforce ... en route to becoming an all graduate profession"* reduces resistance to change.

As eleven of the eighteen participants in my study held managerial positions, a key point highlighted by Interviewee **002** must be considered: *"... usually with health care those who do higher education, you not by bedside but in office."* From my etic point of view, I argue that in time, as more and more nurses attain degrees, there will be limited promotions available and these nurses will be required to provide direct hands-on patient care, as is evident in the UK and Australian health care systems.

Interviewees outlined a conflict between their assumptions and expectations of the TNHE programmes and the assumptions and expectations of the TNHE academics. There were mismatches between western and Malaysian pedagogic and professional values and clinical practices. Associate Professor Dr Hassan, Chairman of the Nursing Education Task Force of the MoHE (2010), confirms that in Malaysia nursing is still influenced by the old British system. Most colleges still use the teacher-centred and didactic approach, whist in clinical settings nurses remain submissive to doctors' orders.

Previously, this was also confirmed by Chiu's (2005, 2006) and Birk's (2005) studies which indicated participants had to bridge from their existing learning mode to a new educational paradigm when studying with international universities. Further, nurses lacked autonomy and empowerment as the practice is task oriented and nursing is still striving to achieve professional status. This resulted in Malaysian nurses perceiving the academics as being unprepared for their TNHE experience. The reported lack of guidance and support for their assessments caused concern and posed difficulties in their classroom experiences and in completing their assessments. The participating nurses reported that western academics' lack of intercultural awareness also led to mis-communication and misunderstanding in the classroom, on-line forums and email exchanges.

Despite the lack of a practice component, it appeared TNHE academics assumed that the nurses would easily translate and demonstrate practical application of the western theory and professional values into local clinical settings. A research undertaken by the MoHE Nursing Task Force on the Basic Nursing Competencies for New Graduates of Diploma Programmes showed that critical thinking to apply the nursing process theory to practice was not taught in the didactic teaching approach in classrooms nor in clinical training (MOHE, 2010). It seemed insufficient consideration had been given to the personal, professional and cultural shifts that nurses would have to make to ensure provision of care was consistent with the culturally different contexts in which that care had to be delivered. This further convinced the nurses of the flying faculty academics' unpreparedness to support the Malaysian nurses.

On completion of the degree, it was evident from the nurses' views that, irrespective of whether they felt learning had taken place or theoretical knowledge could be applied in clinical practice, all acknowledged they had attained a western degree, graduate status, financial reward and enhanced career prospects. Yet again, this confirms that their degrees were undertaken primarily for individualistic and extrinsic reasons.

In spite of many nurses' negative view towards TNHE programmes, with their language and academic difficulties, the nurses demonstrated resilience to the cultural and learning shock of such an intense programme. One such example is their silent behaviour in the classroom. In that silence was the determination and resolve to attain the degree. Following the lectures, they went on-line and researched the topic, worked hard, persevered and conformed to the new learning norms. They started self-help groups to discuss the criteria for assessments and submitted the required work. The nurses appear to have made the necessary adjustments successfully to meet the assessment criteria and achieve their degrees.

It also appeared that certain nurses used their acquired knowledge and their agency in practice. But, there were no clear links as to what coping strategies nurses used that enabled them to internalise what they learnt, nor were there indications as to their ability or motivation to apply or implement some of their learning in practice settings. Neither was there any clear indication as to how far a positive impact of the TNHE knowledge in practice settings would require nurses to make adaptations over the long term and not just in the short-term.

In a theoretical study, Volet and Jones (2012) addressed the issue of the transferability of study approaches from one learning context to another. It concluded that some aspects of student learning transfer well across cultures, while others reflect ambivalent, difficult or inappropriate transfer. This is supported in my study, as certain nurses became strategic in this agency by borrowing almost Anglo-centrically from their association with TNHE programmes. The changes in attitudes, perceptions and decision-making skills from their acquired knowledge increased some nurses' status and power in their practice settings, even amongst doctors.

Having pointed out the lack and inefficacy of TNHE educational preparation to ease cultural conflicts, I now point out that the Australian Vice-Chancellors' Committee (2005) recommendation for cross-cultural training is specifically for TNHE academics. Yet clearly, students have not been considered sufficiently, and neither have the implications of western universities marketing their existing degrees whilst only customising or adapting them to meet certain regulatory frameworks in the receiving countries. Intercultural awareness and sensitivity training for both academics and nurses may make the unknown appear less surprising. Notably, website information for Australian TNHE academics only provides superficial cultural advice and information about politics, values, 'what to do' and 'what not to do' practices. This enables a tourist experience, rather than supporting academics to build links or integrate into local communities. Integration with the community would be a key connecting factor for the intracultural with the intercultural in the TNHE environment (Hawkes, 2010; Knight, 2011, 2010a&b, 2004).

It also seems that there is no recognition that the nurses are studying in their own country, within their national context, and a major challenge lies in breaking with tradition to change beliefs and old habits which are often resistant to change. Further, after the short teaching period, these nurses would return to the same social environment where other professionals, patients and communities still hold those strong cultural values. They also have a responsibility to provide appropriate care for these multicultural, multiracial and multilingual patients in a culturally sensitive manner. I emphasise that relevant care to patient needs can only occur when culture care values are known and serve as the foundation for meaningful care (Leininger, 2011). I also remind the reader of Interviewee **006**'s outlook when the cohort of students recognised the UK academic was totally unaware of the cultural values and ways of Malaysians.

In taking a pragmatic stance some, like Biggs (2014), argue for the TNHE educational experience to be the same as western programmes. He argues that good teaching relies on the universality of the learning process in which the ethnicity of students is largely irrelevant. He stresses this is not the same as devaluing or being dismissive of students' cultures. Others like Mohamad, Rashdan and Rashid, (2006) believe western countries tend to expect eastern students to conform to western models of education which Ziguras (2016), Caruana and Montgomery (2015) and Garrett (2015) identify leads to 'teaching down' to communities that are culturally different from those of the teachers.

A few like Ziguras, 2016; Ziguras and McBurnie, 2015; Hawkes (2010) and Ziguras (2007) believe western academics need to adopt the intercultural educational stance. By rethinking and confronting their beliefs and biases in considering cultural proclivities and linguistic factors, they can connect the intracultural with the intercultural for enhancing students' experiences.

Heffernanan, Morrison, Basu and Sweeney, (2010) argues that TNHE programmes are intentionally chosen in Malaysia based on the assumption that western education and nursing tenets are superior. Adaptations may conflict with MNB, employers' and nurses' expectations whilst also compromising academic standards. Hence, only superficial changes are made by TNHE providers to internationalise the curricula towards Asian countries' social, cultural and educational values (Leask and Carroll, 2011; Wang, 2010). Despite these views, Jin and Cortazzi (2013a&b) point out that students appear to adjust successfully to achieve in their studies after an initial culture and learning shock and acculturation period when they face the new western educational experience.

However, I argue in relation to the six nurses from one UK university where the lack of recognition of their previous experiences led to all nurses failing to meet the assessment criteria. Extra teaching days were then organised to deliver the required academic skills. This has implications for both eastern and western academic standards. The quality of the programme is not assured through following models of knowledge that work in the UK. It also confirms Abdullah's (2010) belief that it is only by understanding unconscious assumptions that people's behaviour can be assessed accurately and appropriate strategies developed to maximise learning.

Participants in my study disagreed with being taught and assessed in the same way as western students. The reasons given were the short-time frame, lack of subject knowledge, differences in classroom culture, education and health care systems. These nurses believed that, as they were in their own country and studying for a foreign degree, the curriculum could be changed to make it meaningful so that what is taught has contemporary relevance; i.e. to internationalise their existing knowledge and skills but still enable them to maintain their national identity and cultural rules. This was to keep them firmly rooted within the Malaysian context. In this sense, the nurses were aligning with Birks, Chapman and Francis (2009) assertion that attempting to achieve 'uniformity of practices' with uncritical imitation and adoption is neither practical nor desirable. This view is further highlighted by Abdullah and Koh (2009) that Malaysians who adopted and practised western values instead of integrating western ways of knowing within Malaysian values were considered culturally ruthless, over-trained and brainwashed.

The dichotomy between the programme as a theory-based degree and participants' ability to link the TNHE knowledge to their everyday clinical practice was evident in the restricted number of examples of how it had influenced care. It also identifies the difficulty to ascertain the extent that TNHE theory was applied in clinical settings and the multi-faceted nature of the issues surrounding the relationship. My findings support Hardwick and Jordan's (2002) study that showed self and professional perspective transformation, but changes in practice and patient outcomes were inconclusive. The data confirms Wenger's (1998) belief that failure of expected learning in each situation still results in learning of another kind. The journeys described are unique to these Malaysian nurses but many issues they raised have been reflected in previous studies in post-registration degree programmes (Chiu, 2005; Birks, 2005).

Questions emerged in relation to the research aim as to why there was an issue with TNHE theoretical knowledge being applied in clinical practice given that patients accept developments in care. Also, why do employers buy into TNHE programmes but resist changes and do not set out strategies to ensure changes are accepted for the best practice that nurses offer them? These questions will be discussed in the next chapter.

The critical thinking, problem-based approach, and reflective skills emphasised in the western approach to nurse education, learned as a nurse and academic, assisted me in writing the academic research text. Critically reviewing in my reflexive journal my beliefs, frustrations and the complexities inherent within cross-cultural experiences of living and studying in a foreign country such as the UK, helped me to provide authenticity. Richardson (2000:929) states "knowing the self and knowing the research subject are intertwined due to historical and local knowledge". Also, as my research progressed, my journal was a useful outlet for my frustrations, challenges, mistakes, successes and differing views. It enabled me to revisit and record an on-going self-appraisal and provided an audit or decision-making trail of the various phases of my research. I also enhanced the rigour of my research approach by exploring how my views changed over the course of undertaking the research.

When writing the text, I questioned whether I selected certain interview extracts to fit my assumptions, as the focus for analysis and interpretation were selected by me as the researcher and interpreter. I point out that although I retained authority over the interpretation of the interview data, the choices I made about including or excluding certain viewpoints and decisions with regards to what data to bring forward were influenced by the selected paradigm, design and methodology, as they only enabled me to inform, rather than dominate, the interpretations. I was able to illuminate the unique voices of these Malaysian nurses by directly using their interview extracts to answer the research question. It confirmed that the insights, values and experiences were influenced by their cultural background. These needed to be made clear in the final text presented to provide an emic and etic view for the reader.

As an insider and outsider to both the Malaysian and British culture, I was empathetic to assumptions within both cultures. But, was confident that, as an insider, I would be able to elicit values revered and upheld by Malaysians. It would enable me to identify, interpret and articulate the similarities and differences in behavioural patterns to enable the reader to understand. Further, it will capture meaning and add value to understanding the nurses' views and experiences of TNHE programmes. Addressing issues arising from these will be beneficial for other Malaysian nurses, TNHE providers, academics, MMoH, MNB, employers who sponsor these programmes and the HE sector. The aim is to show that, although what is taught and the way it is taught may be the same, what is meant may be construed differently due to dissimilar language histories. These may have implications in the TNHE teaching and intercultural classroom environment and application of learning in practice.

The lack of awareness and insight of these 'flying faculty' meant they did not consider the impact of the intense, faster pace, methods of teaching and type of assessments they were offering. Neither did they consider whether the western theory designed to prepare nurses' to function within the western health care system would be able to cross intercultural divides to the culturally influenced Malaysian clinical settings. It is this which is at the heart of the theory-practice divide, the use of formal knowledge instead of ensuring the knowledge base is in line with the realities and needs of Malaysian practice settings (Monaghan, 2015; Scully, 2011; Allan, Smith, O'Driscoll, (2011).

Chapter 5. A Defining moment

Nurses' views of their experiences on TNHE post-registration top-up nursing programmes exposed a gap between Malaysian and western assumptions, expectations, ways, education and health care systems. There was a clash in teaching and learning outlooks, behaviours, assessments and support. In addition, there were the differences in professional values, nursing and patient care practices between nurses and the TNHE 'flying faculty', although all practices are based on WHO standards. The aspects that influenced the application of TNHE theory in clinical practice are illustrated below.

The nurses felt that the TNHE 'flying faculty' had taken a one size fits-all approach with no appreciation of or recognition given to the cultural differences between western and Malaysian teaching and learning and clinical context. This is despite Hall (1976) and Hofstede's (1980) observations of intercultural situations. TNHE 'flying faculty' were unable to provide adequate teaching and support due to the short teaching time-frame. Further, the lack of a practice component also meant they were unable to ensure that nurses learnt and understood the appropriate theory and how to adapt it to Malaysian clinical practice and culture of nursing.

No consideration had been given to Brown's, 2014; Cotterill-Walker's, 2012; Mantzoukas and Jasper's, 2008; Banning's, 2008 arguments that taught theory will enable the ability to perform in the clinical context. Nor was emphasis given to Schober (2013); Leininger (2011) and Birks, Chapman and Francis (2009b) view that theory taught in the classroom must be understood and applicable to practice settings to ensure safe nursing care. This partly contributed to the nurses in this study being unable to apply the TNHE taught theory in practice.

Figure 5.1: Factors determining theory-practice connection

\multicolumn{4}{c}{Factors determining application of TNHE theory in clinical practice}			
TNHE Programmes	Acceptability of nurse-led changes, in practice	(De)Motivating aspects for nurses	MHE, MNB, Employers

Deficits in design
• Lack of cultural considerations
  ○ Teaching time-frame short
  ○ Limited theory
  ○ Language differences
  ○ Teaching & Learning practices
  ○ Professional values
  ○ Clinical practice
  ○ No practice component
  ○ Assumptions and expectations
  ○ Form, quality, standards & qualifications
• Loopholes in Malaysian government regulations
  ○ Lack of guidelines & rules governing TNHE programmes
  ○ Some programmes, no MQA approval
	Relationships
	
	Power/Authority
	Management, Doctors, Senior nurses
	
	+
	
	Junior nurses
	
	+
	
	• Resources
	• Environment
	• Patients
		Motivation:
		• Self-identity as professionals; responsible and accountable.
		Demotivation
		• Fast-track learning
		• Assessment focused mode
		• Less support than expected
		• Lack of understanding
		• Theory to practice gap
		• Their prerogative whether apply theory-practice
		• How and to what extent
		• Priorities/incentives had been:
		  - Status of western degree
		  - Financial
		  - Promotion
		  - Ability for further study
			Degree of commitment to nurse-led changes:
			
			• Focus on
			  - Award of Western degree
			  - Organisational reputations/ Western-associated status
			  - Local institutional ranking systems
			
			• Lack of institutional follow-up guidance, structure, organisation, support post TNHE delivery for nurses to implement change in practice.

Much has been written regarding the differences between western and eastern cultures (Wang, 2010; Selmer and Lauring, 2010), in education (Bickmore, Hayhoe, Manion, Mundy, and Read, 2016; Montgomery, 2016; Hassan and Jamaludin, 2010) and health care systems (Finston, 2017; Smullen and Phua, 2015; Mandel, 2009). However, none of those differences, nor the short teaching time-frame of one to two weeks using western-based academic content, learning outcomes and assessments with no practice component deterred the MHE or the MNB from accepting the offered TNHE programmes. Nor did the lack of MQA recognition of some of the programmes cause any concern. There appeared to be no detrimental implications for nurses deriving from this decision as they were still entitled to benefit from the financial incentive and opportunities for promotion and further study.

The post-registration top-up nursing degree programmes of study offered by the three western universities all varied in their form, quality and standards. Variations existed because of loopholes in the Malaysian government regulations, and the lack of clear guidelines and rules governing the TNHE degree programmes. Thus, all three TNHE providers could bypass some of the stipulated regulations and provide programmes as they saw fit.

During their study on the programme, the Malaysian nurses' experiences were painful and challenging. They had to fast-track their learning in an assessment-focused mode with far less support than expected. Their desire to succeed spurred them on to overcome the resulting culture and learning shock by using effective coping strategies. However, the financial incentive, increased chances of career progression through promotion, and the valuable qualities that inspired them to achieve the degree, had only a minimal effect on their motivation and ability to make and sustain changes in practice. The question it raises is whether this was because the taught theory was not allied to the practice settings in Malaysia? Interestingly, it underlines the reasons stated by Birks, Chapman and Francis (2009a); Egan and Jaye (2009) and Flanagan (2009) that taught theory must be relevant to clinical settings.

Muir and Laxton (2012), Cathro (2011) and Bellfield and Gessner (2010) stress that the theory-practice connection is vital in the provision of quality care. However, due to conflicting views and limited number of examples given by the nurses, it was not possible to determine the extent to which TNHE theoretical knowledge was applied by them in clinical settings. It also highlighted the difficulty of ascertaining if and how theory and practice are connected. It remained the nurses' prerogative to decide whether they wanted to apply their learning in clinical settings, how they did so and to what extent.

One major flaw in getting TNHE theory to contribute to changes in clinical settings, or to impact on the provision of patient care, could be that neither the TNHE 'flying faculty', the Malaysian Ministry of Health, the MHE, MNB nor employers offered any guidance, support or experiential learning to achieve this. Organisational and environmental factors, resistance to change, lack of acceptance of changes and the apparent resentment shown towards graduate and honours graduate status also impeded any opportunity to bridge the theory-practice gap.

The interview data reflected the voices of the TNHE nurses who, in their personal quest to achieve a degree, indirectly helped to meet the TNHE providers' aim to obtain and fulfil their income-generating contracts, and raise their international profile and influence in Malaysia. Private hospital employers who funded the programmes could upgrade their nurse managers and nurses to graduate status, and thereby raise their organisation's ranking by employing western-taught graduates. The Ministry of Health's goal to improve the nursing workforce to graduate status by offering a financial incentive helped to raise the percentage of nurses with degrees. MNB's aims for part-time post-registration top-up nursing degrees to upgrade diploma nurses, attain a western degree at reduced costs and improve CPE opportunities were also attained (MNB, 2008). Vision 2020's objective to enable Malaysia to achieve a developed country status through its graduate level workforce also appears to have been advanced, and is on way to being met.

Agendas of key stakeholders above appear generally to be met, directly or indirectly, apart from the Government's 2020 agenda of changing the mind-set of nurses. The Malaysian Ministry of Health's anticipation that nurses would utilise western expertise and innovation to enhance standards of care, and MNB's objective to improve patient care, were not fully met. In other words, everybody appeared to win except the patients.

The nurses stated that in Malaysia, TNHE programmes from western countries are considered superior in credibility, integrity and expertise, and are a status symbol compared to programmes offered by local universities. However, shortcomings in the TNHE teaching and learning environment and the theory-practice gap led to participants questioning the validity of the programmes.

Despite all the differences and nurse-reported shortcomings, the TNHE programmes do appear to have had transformational effects on the nurses' relationships with aspects of learning and clinical practice. The programme empowered them (Aiken, Rafferty and Sermeus, 2014; Birks, Chapman and Francis, 2009b, Darbyshire, 2006), enhanced their confidence (Brown, 2014; Ng, Tuckett, Fox-Young, Kain (2014); Chong, Sellick, Francis, Abdullah, 2011; Lillibridge and Fox's, 2005; Davey and Robinson, 2002), and improved their intellectual, information technology and critical thinking skills, thus enabling them to portray themselves more positively (Watkins and Ryan, 2015; Ling, Mazzolini and Giridharan, 2014; Birks, Chapman and Francis, 2009a&b; Chiu, 2005).

The adjustment and adaptations the nurses made during, and because of, their TNHE experiences is demonstrated. Their ways of knowing changed as they became drawn to read, learn and research even though during their degree programme they had difficulty in comprehending the new theory. These nurses have now become part of a new community of practice within the Malaysian post-registration top-up nursing degree, health care system and society.

Recommendations

The nurses' previous spoon-fed, or teacher-centred and exam focused style of learning led to cultural and learning shock. Their resilience and coping strategies enabled them to adjust to complete the intense westernised programme. This demonstrates that learning styles are contextually rather than culturally based. It also raises a key point, i.e. although an individual can adopt new ideas, values and modes of teaching and learning, it takes time to adjust and adapt.

In TNHE programmes delivered in Malaysia, the short teaching time-frame restricts nurses' ability to adapt to UK and Australian HE styles of teaching and learning. Other factors such as lack of a practice component, differences in assumptions, expectations, outlook in the classroom and professional ways of working in practice resulted in a lack of expected impact on patient care. Also, it appears that TNHE providers, MMoH, MHE, MNB, universities, employers and nurses all focused on the degree award itself, rather than the existing structure or organisation to ensure that what was learnt was taken forward into practice.

If the design and delivery of these TNHE programmes is improved, in addition to nurses' personal and professional development, clear evidence-based practice methods could be developed. This is apparent from some of the extracts that demonstrate application of TNHE theory in practice despite the factors that were working against it. It is not surprising, given these factors, that nurses did not acknowledge an uptake of TNHE theory. Nevertheless, the contradictions between their accounts suggest there was some uptake. Over time, this uptake could either diminish or develop with additional nursing experience, post TNHE.

Reflecting on the study

The title "A defining moment" for my research was chosen because verbatim extracts of nurses' unique voices were used to speak, i.e. to represent, their difficult experiences in the TNHE classroom environment during the short, intensive teaching time-frame. It also explains their experiences in practice settings, and the level of instrumentality and motivation, and emotional and psychological adjustment these nurses undertook to attain successfully their western degrees. I took Skeggs' (2002) advice to use reflexivity to examine power and responsibility within the research. Self-experiences and personal, professional and researcher stances were integrated to provide knowledge and make claims to empower and create meaning.

Initially, during the interviews, participants gave reserved responses to questions due to my perceived outsider status as a UK academic. My insider knowledge allowed me to slip effortlessly into a Malaysian insider role. I used Bahasa Malaysia, colloquial words and humour to cajole them to disclose detailed accounts (Merleau-Ponty, 1962). I also revealed my personal experiences as an international student nurse to create a persona that would encourage a more confidential, detailed and revealing account.

My insider and outsider viewpoints will enable the reader to appreciate the nurses' outlook and values whilst interviews may have provided a degree of security for the nurses in which to reveal their private or hidden transcripts (Scott, 1996). I do not believe they would have disclosed certain details in the same way with an outsider or non-Malaysian.

This confirmed that the emic position and safe place for disclosure are hidden dilemmas decided on only by the participants (Beoku-Betts, 1994). Using my insider Malaysian insights, I stress that these findings may not correlate with the module evaluations that the nurses provided at the end of the short period of face-to-face or on-line teaching of a module. This is because of the tendency for Malaysian nurses to provide more socially acceptable responses in order to save face, both of self and authority. Further, they may have feared negative consequences, such as being perceived as having a bad image, or being subjected to reprisals.

The research carried out here resonates with the suggestions from Race (2011; 2013) and Burton and Kirshbaum (2012) that attention needs to be directed to identifying and working with cultural differences in Western teaching and learning relationships with international students. The contribution my study makes to this assertion is to have found what those cultural differences appear to mean within the Malaysian nursing context. I have explored overlapping layers of these cultural differences in teaching and learning, social aspects, educational system and professional values and attitudes.

Suggested further research

TNHE is currently developing fast in Asian countries, including Malaysia, Sri Lanka, China and Singapore. It is a fact evidenced at the 3rd International Conference of Teaching and Learning (International University, 2011) where the interim results of this study were presented (McIver and Arunasalam, 2011).

My findings suggest further research focusing on a longitudinal study looking at the degree of impact of taught knowledge in clinical practice after one year, two years and four years post-TNHE post-registration nursing programmes. This would provide evidence of the long-term impact on nurses and their practice, to inform both the Malaysian government and TNHE providers. It assumes that all stakeholders and participants wish to move beyond their short-term gains into the area of actually maintaining CPE, personal and professional transformations, theory-practice connections and improving patient care.

A further area for research is to determine why certain nurses could internalise what they learnt in TNHE programmes. What was it that motivated them to make the theory-practice connection in the care of patients?

Another line of research that is directly suggested by my findings is to identify why employers are now resisting the changes for best practice that these nurses are offering them. The employers had intentionally collaborated with TNHE providers to provide these programmes for their staff development. Such research may identify strategies that would be suitable to ensure that others are more accepting of changes proposed, planned and implemented.

Contribution of this research

This book addresses the gap in research where the voice of the offshore student *"is conspicuously missing from the research literature"* (Chapman and Pyvis, 2005: 40). The unique insights found through listening to nurses' own voices, outline their personal and professional transformations which led them to succeed (through conflicts, struggles, experiences, adjustment, adaptation and successes) and become part of a new community of nurses.

Previous studies undertaken in Malaysia by a combination of insiders, insider/outsider (like me) and outsiders, using questionnaires, or semi-structured interviews, or semi-structured interviews and focus groups all showed that nurses' motivations to undertake post-registration programmes were for personal and professional development and to improve practice and patient care.

Their data indicated that the attainment of knowledge had led to positive changes in practice and enhanced patient care.

In contrast, my research demonstrates that the key motivators of nurses to undertake TNHE programmes were their desire to get a high status western degree, financial incentives and future promotion. Basically, individualistic and extrinsic reasons rather than application of theory in practice or enhancement of patient care. Therefore, I ask the reader to consider the findings of previous studies in relation to the outlook of nurses in my study on completing questionnaires, their spoken English, the concept of saving face of self and others, and the perceived threats inherent in voicing their opinions to westerners.

My role as a UK-based Malaysian nurse academic instigated this study. I attempted to put forward insider and outsider standpoints to interpret Malaysian nurses' views on the extent to which they have applied TNHE theoretical knowledge in clinical settings. It enabled me to illuminate western TNHE as delivered in Malaysia, from Malaysian nurses' perspectives. The findings revealed the elevated status accorded to western degrees by these Malaysian nurses, and what they experienced when studying TNHE programmes and in clinical practice. It is worth noting that improving the education, role, professionalism and status of nurses and the nursing profession may not equate to improving the overall standard of patient care, unless implementation of new practice in the provision of patient care is directly addressed.

Conclusion

This book is based on research that has provided a platform for Malaysian nurses' unique voices to be heard reflecting on TNHE post-registration top-up nursing degree programmes. It enables readers to recognise that, while partnerships and collaborations appear to be ways forward, it is important that Nurse Education universities identify and consider relevant strategies to overcome the challenges that nurses and 'flying faculty' academics both face.

It is a useful tool for MNB as it will help them to select TNHE programmes that promote nurse education, transform healthcare delivery approaches and ensure improvements in the provision of patient care. The data is also relevant to all those engaged in international collaboration and higher education, including other professions, and all TNHE programmes delivered in Malaysia and in other South East Asian countries, where strong cultural factors continue to affect society.

Competition between HEIs is being compounded by world economic downturns. These top-up degree programmes are marketing advantages for Western TNHE providers due to the perceptions in some Asian countries of the elevated status of western degrees. These are advantages that are being exploited now in a way they may not have been in the past. The lines between what is ethical and effectual, and what is not, may be blurring under the current economic pressures on HEIs to compete abroad.

References

Abdullah, A., (2010). Culture Influences on Learning and Thinking. October 10th Presentation at Seri Pacific Hotel. Kuala Lumpur.

Abdullah, A. and Koh, SL., (2009). Culture Matters in Malaysia. Kuala Lumpur. Pearson Prentice Hall.

Abdullah, A. and Pedersen, P., (2003). Understanding Multicultural Malaysia. Kuala Lumpur, Malaysia. Pearson Prentice Hall.

Agar, M., (2011). Making Sense of One Other for Another: Ethnography as Translation. Language and Communication. 31. 38-47.

Ahmad, F., Shah, P. and Aziz, S., (2005). Choice of Teaching Methods: Teacher-centred or Student-centred. *Journal Penyelidikan Pendidikan*. 7.57-74.

Ahmed, S., (2000). Strange Encounters: Embodied Others in Post-Coloniality (Transformations). New York and London. Routledge.

Aiken, L., Rafferty, A.M. and Sermeus, W., (2014). Caring nurses hit by a quality storm: Low investment and excessive workloads, not uncaring attitudes, are damaging the image of NHS trusts, argue the authors of ground breaking research into Europe's nurse workforce. *Nursing Standard*. 28(35). 22-25.

Alavi, K., Sail R.M., Idris, K., Samah, A.A., Omar, M., (2011). Living arrangement preference and family relationship expectation of elderly parents. *Pertanika Journal of Social Science and Humanities* 19. 65-73.

Ales, P,. (2010). The language medium policy in Malaysia: A plural society model? *Review of European Studies*. 2(2).

Alexander, H., (2010). Upper Secondary Male Students' Perception of Nursing as a Career Choice. *International Journal for the Advancement of Science and Arts*. 1(1). 46-62.

Ali, H., (2008). *The Malays*. Malaysia. The Other Press.

Allan, T.H., Smith, P., and O'Driscoll, M., (2011). Experiences of supernumerary status and the hidden curriculum in nursing: a new twist in the theory–practice gap?. *Journal of Clinical Nursing*. 20. 847–855.

Altbach, P.G. and Knight, J., (2006). The internationalization of higher education: Motivations and realities. *NEA Almanac of Higher Education*. 7-36. Washington. National Education Association.

Amir, S., (2009). The influence of national culture on communication practices: A case study on Malaysian Organisation. Masters dissertation. Queensland University of Technology.

Anderson, L. E., (1994). A new look at an old construct: cross-cultural adaptation. *International Journal of Intercultural Relations*. 18. 293-328.

Arif, S., Ilyas, M. and Hameed, A., (2013). Student Satisfaction and Impact of Leadership in Private Universities. *The TQM Journal*. 25(4). 399-416.

Arunasalam, N.D., (2009). Learning To Teach in Culturally Different and Appropriate Ways. Unpublished paper. University of Hertfordshire.

Australian Nursing and Midwifery Board (1981) Health Practitioner Regulation National Law. State and territorial nursing regulation authorities. NMBA.

Australian Nursing Council, (1994). National competency standards for the registered nurse and the enrolled nurse in Recommended Domains. Sydney. ANC.

Australian Nursing and Midwifery Accreditation Council, (2010). National Accredtation Guidelines. Canberra City, Australia. ANMAC.

Australian Nursing and Midwifery Accreditation Council, (2012). National Accreditation Guidelines. Canberra City, Australia. ANMAC.

Australian Nursing and Midwifery Council, (2009). Practice Standards. Australia. ANMC.

Australian Qualifications Framework, (2002). Implementation Handbook. (3^{rd}ed.). Carlton, South Victoria. AQF Advisory Board.

Australian Vice – Chancellors' Committee, (2003). Offshore Programs of Australian Universities: Offshore Programs Conducted under Formal Agreements between Australian Universities and Overseas Higher Education Institutions or Organisations. Canberra. Australian Vice-Chancellors' Committee.

Bakar, H.A., and Mustaffa, C.S., (2013). Organizational communication in Malaysia organizations: Incorporating cultural values in communication scale, Corporate Communications: An International Journal. 18(1). 87-109.

Banning, M., (2008). A review of clinical decision making: models and current research. Journal of Clinical Nursing. 17(2). 187-95.

Barnett, T., Namasivayam, P. and Narudin, D.A.A., (2010). A critical review of the nursing shortage in Malaysia. International Nursing Review. 32-39.

Belenky, M. F, Clinchy, B.M, Goldberger, N.R. and Tarule, J. M., (1986). Women's Ways of Knowing. New York. Harper Collins.

Bennett, P., Bergen, S., Cassar, D., Hamilton, M., Soinila, M., Sursock, A. and Williams, P., (2010). Quality assurance in transnational higher education (Report). 1-38. Helsinki, Finland. The European Association for Quality Assurance in Higher Education.

Bellfield, S. and Gessner, G., (2010). Factors influencing advancement of professional education of nurses. MSc thesis. Washington. Georgetown University.

Beoku-Betts, J., (1994). When black is not enough: doing field research among Gullah women. NWSA Journal. 6 (3). 413-433.

Beoku-Betts, J., (2004). African women pursuing graduate studies in the sciences: racism, gender bias, and third world marginality. NWSA Journal. 16. 116-135.

Berry, J. W., (2005). Acculturation: Living successfully in two cultures. International Journal of Intercultural Relation. 29. 697-712.

Bickmore, K., Hayhoe, R., Manion, C., Mundy, K. and Read, R., (2016). Comparative and International Education: Issues for Teachers. Toronto. Canadian Scholars Press.

Biggs, J., (2014). Constructive alignment in university teaching. HERDSA Review of Higher Education. 1. 5-22.

Birks, M., (2005). The impact of post-registration degree studies on nurses in Malaysian Borneo – Challenges and changes. University Malaysia International Nursing Research Conference: Quality Nursing Practice through Research. Sheraton Subang Hotel and Towers, Subang Jaya, Selangor Darul Ehsan. 29th-30th August.

Birks, M., (2006). Supporting the evolution of a research culture among nurses in Malaysia. Australian Journal of Advanced Nursing. 27(1): 87-93.

Birks, M., Chapman, Y. and Francis, K., (2007). Breaching the wall: Interviewing people from other cultures. Journal of Transcultural Nursing. 18(2). 150-156.

Birks, M., Chapman, Y., and Francis, K., (2009a). Women and Nursing in Malaysia. Journal of Transcultural Nursing. 20. 116-123.

Birks, M., Chapman, Y., Francis, K., (2009b). Becoming different: perspective transformation through post-registration baccalaureate nursing studies. Book Chapter. New York. Nova.

Bista, K., (2011). Learning-Centered Community College and English as a Second Language Programme. The Southeast Asian Journal of English Language Studies. 17(1). 113 – 121.

Blackman, S. and Kempson, M., (2016). *The Subcultural Imagination: Theory, Research and Reflexivity in Contemporary Youth Cultures (Youth, Young Adulthood and Society)*. Oxon. Routledge.

Bligh, D. A., (2000). What's the use of lectures? San Francisco. Jossey-Bass.

Boland, G., Sugahara, S., Opdecam, E. and Everaert, P., (2011). The impact of cultural factors on students' learning style preferences. Asian Review of Accounting. 19(3). 243-265.

Bone, D., (2008). Internationalisation of HE: A Ten Year View. Report prepared for DIUS. The Debate on the Future of Higher Education.

Bone, D., (2009). Internationalisation of HE: A Ten Year View. Report prepared for DIUS. The Debate on the Future of Higher Education.

Boore, J., (1996). Postgraduate Education in Nursing: A case study. Journal of Advanced Nursing. 23(3): 620-629.

Bowers, B., (2009). Student nurses should not underestimate the value of delivering hands-on, personal care. Nursing Times. Practice Comment.

Bridges, W., (2013). Managing Transitions. United Kingdom. Da Capo Press.

Brown, V., (2014). The Experience of Post-qualifying Healthcare Students of University-based Continuing Professional Development. Doctorate in Professional Studies. Leeds Beckett University.

Brown, L. and Holloway, I., (2008). The Initial Stage of the International Sojourn: Excitement or Culture Shock? *British Journal of Guidance and Counselling.* 36 (1). 33-49.

Bryant, S., (2017). The meaning of silence in different cultures. USA. Country Navigator.

Burns, N. and Grove, S.K., (2008). Understanding nursing research: Building and evidence-based practice. St Louis. Saunders Elsevier.

Burton, R., (2009). Nursing Beyond the Horizon. Education Matters. The Malaysian Journal of Nursing. August.

Burton, R and Kirshbaum, M., (2012). Curriculum Considerations for International Students on Professional Doctorate Courses: A Perspective from the United Kingdom. In: 3rd International Conference on Professional Doctorates: ICPD 3, 2-3 April, Italy. European University Institute.

Byram, M., (1997). Teaching and Assessing Intercultural Communicative Competence. Clevedon. Multilingual Matters Ltd.

Carr, P.R., (2012). Debating Language, Culture, Race and Power: Is There A Difference Between Interculturalism and Multiculturalism? in H.K.Wright et al (Eds.). Precarious International Multicultural Education: Hegemony, Dissent and Rising Alternatives. 277-296. The Netherlands. Sense Publishers.

Caruana, V. and Montgomery, C., (2015). Understanding the transnational higher education landscape: Shifting positionality and the complexities of partnership. *Learning and Teaching.* 8 (1). 5-29.

Cathro H., (2011). Pursuing graduate studies in nursing education: driving and restraining Forces. The Online Journal of Issues in Nursing. 16(3).

Cerroni-Long, E.L., (1994). Insider and Outsider Perspectives in the Study of Ethnicity: The Case of the Italian-American. Ethnic Forum. 14 (Spring). 121–38.

Chaboyer, W. and Retsas, A., (1996). Critical Care Graduate Diploma: Nursing Students Needs Identified in Evaluation. Australian Critical Care. 9 (1).15-19.

Chapman, A. and Pyvis, D., (2005). Identity and social practice in higher education: student experiences of postgraduate courses delivered "offshore" in Singapore and Hong Kong by an Australian university'. International Journal of Educational Development. 25(1). 39–52.

Chasseguet-Smirgel, J., (1976). Some Thoughts on the Ego Ideal. Psychoanalytic Quarterly. 45. 345-373.

Chee, H. L. and Barraclough, S., (2007). Health Care in Malaysia: The Dynamics of Provision, Financing and Access. Oxon. Routledge.

Chiarella, M., (2002). The Legal and Professional Status of Nurses. Edinburgh, Scotland. Churchill Livingstone.

Chiu, L.H., (2005). Motivation for Nurses Undertaking Post-registration Qualification in Malaysia. International Nursing Review. 52 (1). 46-51.

Chiu, L., (2006). Malaysian Registered Nurses' Professional Learning. International Journal of Nursing Education Scholarship. 3. 1-12.

Chong, E. M., Sellick, K., Francis, K. and Abdullah, K.L., (2011). What Influences Malaysian Nurses to Participate in Continuing Professional Education Activities? Asian Nursing Research. 5 (1).

Chong, M.C., Francis, K., Cooper, S. and Abdullah, K.L., (2014). Current Continuing Professional Education Practice among Malaysian Nurses. Nursing Research Practice. Jan 9.

Chong, M. C., (2013). Understanding the continuing professional education needs among Malaysian Nurses and their readiness for e-learning. Ph.D. thesis, Monash University, Melbourne, Australia.

Chuang, S., (2012). The relationship between cultural values and learning preference: the impact of acculturation experiences upon East Asians. International Journal of Training and Development. 16(1).

Cochran-Smith, M. and Lytle, S. (1999). Relationship of knowledge and practice: Teacher learning in communities. In A. Iran-Nejad and C. D. Pearson (Eds.), Review of research in education 24. 249-306. Washington. American Educational Research Association.

Cohen, D. and Gunz, A., (2002). As seen by the other...Perspectives on the self in the memories and emotional perceptions of Easterners and Westerners. Psychological Science 13. 55-59.

Constitution of Malaysia, (1957). Article 160; Retrieved June 26, 2017 from http://confinder.richmond.edu/admin/docs/malaysia.pdf.

Cooley, M., (2008). Nurses' Motivations for Studying Third Level Post-registration Nursing Programmes and the Effects of Studying on their Personal and Work Lives. Nurse Education Today. 28 (5). 588-594.

Coomarasamy J. D., Wint N. and Sukumaran S., (2015). Prevalence of Obesity and Daily Lifestyles of the Registered Nurses in Malaysia. International Journal of Innovation and Applied Studies. 7(3). 1202–1208.

Cotterill-Walker, S.M., (2012). Where is the evidence that master's level nursing education makes a difference to patient care? A literature review. Nurse Education Today. 32(1). 57-64.

Creswell, J. W., and Clark, V. L.P., (2011). Designing and conducting mixed methods research (2nd ed.). Thousand Oaks, CA: Sage.

Crichton, J. A., Paige, M., Papademetre, L. and Scarino, A., (2004). Integrated Resources for Intercultural Teaching and Learning in the Context of Internationalisation in Higher Education. University of South Australia. Research Centre for Languages and Cultures Education.

Crismore, A., (2003). An American Woman Teaching in Malaysia: Remembering the Obstacles and Successes. Journal of Adolescent and Adult Literacy. 46 (5). 380.

Cronin, P. and Rawlings, A.K., (2004). Knowledge for Contemporary nursing practice. Edinburgh. Mosby Co.

Currie, G., and Knights, D., (2003). Reflecting on a critical pedagogy in MBA education. Management Learning. 34(1). 27-49.

Darbyshire, P., (2006). Heroines, Hookers and Harridans: Exploring popular images and representations of nurses and nursing. In Speedy, S., Daly, J., and Jackson, D., (Eds.). 189-202. Contexts of nursing: An introduction. Sydney, Australia. Elsevier.

Davey, B. and Robinson, S., (2002). Taking a Degree after Qualifying as a Registered General Nurse: Constraints and Effects. Nurse Education Today. 22 (8). 624-31.

Davidson, M., (2013). Culture Shock, Learning Shock and Re-entry Shock. Academic Development Advisor. PESL.

Dearing R., (1997). Report of the National Committee of Inquiry into Higher Education. London, HMSO.

Delaney, C. and Piscopo, B. (2004). RN-BSN Programs: Associate Degree and Diploma Nurses' Perceptions of the Benefits and Barriers to Returning to School. Journal for Nurses in Staff Development. 20 (4). 157-16.

Dema, O., and Moeller, A. K., (2012). Teaching culture in the 21st century language classroom. Faculty Publications: Department of Teaching, Learning and Teacher Education. 181.

Denscombe, M., (2007). The Good Research Guide for Small-Scale Social Research Projects. Berkshire. Open University Press.

Denzin, N. K., Lincoln, Y. S., (2011). The SAGE Handbook of Qualitative Research. Thousand Oaks. SAGE Publications.

Des Jardin, K.E., (2001). Political Involvement in Nursing – Education and Empowerment.... First in a series of two articles. AORN Journal. 74 (4). 467-471.

Dooley, G., (1990). The Transfer of Australian Nursing Education from Hospitals to Tertiary Institutions : An Annotated Bibliography. Bedford Park, S. Australia. South Australian College of Advanced Education Library.

Dowswell, T., Hewison, J. and Hinds, M., (1998). Motivational Forces Affecting Participation in Post-registration Degree Course and Effects on Home and Work Life: A Qualitative Study. Journal of Advanced Nursing. 28 (6). 1326-1333.

Dugdall, H., (2009). What is the relationship between nurses' attitude to evidence based. Journal of Clinical Nursing. 18(10). 1442-50.

Dugdall, H. Watson, R., (2009). What is the relationship between nurses' attitude to evidence based practice and the selection of wound care procedures? Journal of Clinical Nursing. 18(10). 1442-50.

Dumont, L., (1986). Essays on individualism. Chicago. University of Chicago Press.

Dunn, L. and Wallace, M., (2008). Teaching in Transnational Higher Education. Oxon: Routledge.

Durkin, K., (2004). The Middle Way: Exploring Differences in Academic Expectations. Perceptions of Critical Thinking of East Asian Students in the UK. Paper presented at the International Conference on New Directions in the Humanities. Tuscany.

Dyess, S.M. and Chase, S.K., (2012). Sustaining health in faith community nursing practice: Emerging processes that support the development of a middle-range theory. Holistic Nursing Practice. 26 (4). 221-7.

Egan, T. and Jaye, C., (2009). Communities of clinical practice: the social organisation of clinical learning. Health: An Interdisciplinary Journal for the Social Study of Health, Illness and Medicine. 13(1). 107-125.

Egege, S. and Kutieleh, S., (2004). Critical thinking: Teaching Foreign Notions to Foreign Students. International Education Journal: Educational Research Conference. Special Issue. 4(4). 75-85.

Eraut, M., (2004). Informal Learning in the Workplace. Studies in Continuing Education. 26: 247-273.

Esmond, P., and Sandwich, E., (2004). Letter to the Editor: Entry Into Practice: Is It Relevant Today? Nurse Education Today. April.

Etherington, K., (2004). Becoming a Reflexive Researcher. London. Jessica Kingsley.

Finston, P., (2017). Why are Eastern and Western Treatments so Different? Soul IS on the Sick List. Acu-Psychiatry. Bi-Monthly Blog to Raise Awareness.

Finlay, L., (2003). The reflexive journey: mapping multiple routes. In L. Finlay and B. Gough (Eds.), Reflexivity: A Practical Guide for Researchers in Health and Social Sciences. 3-20. Oxford. Blackwell.

Fiske, S. T., (1989). Examining the Role of Intent: Toward Understanding Its Role in Stereotyping and Prejudice. In Uleman J.S., and Bargh, J.A., (Eds). Unintended Thought. 253-283. New York. Guilford Press.

Fitch, K. and Surma, A., (2006). The Challenges of International Education: Developing a Public Relations Unit for the Asian Region. Journal of University Teaching and Learning Practice. 3(2). 104-113.

Flanagan, J., (2009). Patient and nurse experiences of theory-based care. Nursing Science Quarterly. 22(2). 160-72.

Fontaine, R. and Richardson, S., (2005). Cultural values in Malaysia: Chinese, Malays and Indians compared. Cross Cultural Management: An International Journal. 12(4). 63-77.

Furnham, A., (1997). The Experience of Being an Overseas Student. In McNamara, D., and Harris, R. (Eds). Overseas Students in Higher Education. 13-29. London. Routledge.

Furnham, A., (2004). Foreign students - Education and culture shock. Psychologist, 17(1). 16-19.

Gagliardi, S. and Mazor, K.M., (2007). Student decisions about lecture attendance: do electronic course materials matter? Academic Medicine. 82(10). Supplement: S73-6.

Garrett, R., (2015). The Rise and Fall of Transnational Higher Education in Singapore. International Higher Education. Globalization currents. 9.

Gaw, K.F., (2000). Reverse Culture Shock in Students Returning From Overseas. International Journal of Intercultural Relations. 24(1). 83-104.

Geertz, C., (1973). The Interpretation of Cultures: Selected Essays. New York. Basic Books.

Gergen, K., (1999). An Invitation to Social Construction. London. SAGE.

Gijbels, H., O'Connell, R., Dalton-O'Connor, C. and O'Donovan, M., (2010). A Systematic Review Evaluating the Impact of Post-registration Nursing and Midwifery Education on Practice. Nurse Education in Practice.

Gill, J., (2009). Malaysia: Full of Western promise. The times higher education. Retrieved July, 4, 2017 from http//:www.timeshighereducation.co.uk/story.asp?storycode.

Gill, S.K., (2009). Language Education Policy in Multi-Ethnic Malaysia. In The Routledge International Companion to Multicultural Education. Banks, J.A. 397-409. New York. Routledge/Taylor and Francis.

Giroux, H. A. (2010) 'Bare Pedagogy and the Scourge of Neoliberalism: Rethinking Higher Education as a Democratic Public Sphere', The Educational Forum. 74. 184-196.

Glass, J. C., (1998). The Contested Workplace: Reactions to Hospital Based RNs Doing Degrees. Collegian. 5(1). 24-31.

Goffman, E., (1959). The Presentation of Self in Everyday Life. New York. Doubleday.

Gould, D., Drey, N. and Berridge, E., (2007). Nurses' experiences of Continuing Professional Development. Nurse Education Today. 27(6). 602-609.

Gribben, M., McLellan, S. and Mc Girr, D., (2017). *How to Survive your Nursing or Midwifery Course*. London. SAGE Publications Ltd.

Griscti O, Jacono J (2006) Effectiveness of continuing education programmes in nursing: literature review. *Journal of Advanced Nursing*. 55(4). 449-56.

Griffiths, D.S., Winstanley, D. and Gabriel, Y. (2004). Learning Shock - The Trauma of Return to Formal Learning. Tanaka Business School Discussion papers. London: Tanaka Business School.

Grotevant, H.D., (1992). Assigned and Chosen Identity Components: A Process Perspective on their Integration. In Adams, G.R., Montemayor, R., and Gulotta,T., (Eds). Advances in Adolescent Development. 4. 73-90. Newbury Park, CA. SAGE.

Hardwick, S., and Jordan, S., (2002). The Impact of Part-Time Post-registration Degrees on Practice. *Journal of Advanced Nursing*. 38(5). 524-535.

Haddock, G., and Maio, G.R., (2007). "Attitudes" In Encyclopaedia of Social Psychology. California. SAGE.

Hall, E. T., (1976). Beyond Culture. Garden City, New York. Anchor.

Hammersley, M., (2012). Methodological Paradigms in Educational Research. British Educational Research Association on-line resource.

Hardwick, S., and Jordan, S., (2002). The Impact of Part-Time Post-registration Degrees on Practice. Journal of Advanced Nursing. 38(5): 524-535.

Harris, M., (1968). The Rise of Anthropological Theory: A History of Theories of Culture. Oxford. Rowman and Littlefield Publishers Inc.

Hashim, F. and Abas, N., (2000). English Teaching in Malaysia. TESOL. Matters. Feb/Mar.

Hassan, A. and Jamaludin, N.S., (2010). Approaches and values in two gigantic educational philosophies: East and West. Selangor, Malaysia. University Putra Malaysia.

Hassan, H. (2010). Development of Nursing Education in Malaysia towards the year 2020. Department of Higher Education, Ministry of Health Malaysia. Shah Alam. University Publication Centre (UPENA).

Hawkes, D., (2010). *The relative importance of nature, nurture and peer effects on adult outcomes: Full research report ESRC end of award report, RES-000-22-1545*. Project Report. Swindon. ESRC.

Healey, N.M., (2015b). The challenges of leading an international branch campus: the 'lived experience' of in-country senior managers. Journal of Studies in International Education. 26 August.

Heffernanan, T., Morrison, M., Basu, P. and Sweeney, A. (2010). Cultural differences, learning styles and transnational education. Journal of Higher Education Policy and Management. 32(1). 27-39.

Helms, R.M., (2008). Transnational Education in China: Key Challenges, Critical Issues and Strategies for Success. London. The Observatory on Borderless Higher Education.

Hellsten, M. and Prescott, A., (2004). Learning at University: The International Student Experience. International Education Journal. 5(3).

Higginson, R., (2006). Fears, worries and experiences of first year pre-registration nursing students: a qualitative study. Nurse Researcher. 13(3). 32-49.

Hill, C., Cheong, K.C., Leong Y.C. and Fernandez-Chung, R., (2014). TNE – Transnational education or tensions between national and external? A case study of Malaysia. Studies in Higher Education 39(6). 952-66.

Hishamshah, M., Rashid, A., Mustaffa, W., Haroon, R. and Badaruddin, N., (2011). Belief and Practices of Traditional Post Partum Care Among a Rural Community in Penang Malaysia. The Internet Journal Third World Medicine. 9(14).

Hofstede, G., (1980). Culture's Consequences: International Differences in Work Related Values. Beverly Hills, CA. SAGE Publications.

Hofstede, G., (1984). Culture's Consequences: International Differences in Work Related Values. Newbury, CA. SAGE Publications.

Hofstede, G., (1991). Culture's Consequences: International Differences in Work Related Values. Beverley Hills, CA. SAGE.

Hofstede, G., (2001). Culture's Consequences: Comparing Values, Behaviors, Institutions, and Organisations across Nations (2nd ed.). Thousand Oaks, CA. SAGE Publications.

Hogan, R., (2012.) Transnational Distance Learning and Building New Markets for Universities. University of South Pacific, Fiji. IGI Global.

Hunt, J., (2013). Nurses must spend a year on basic care. Nursing Times. 26 March.

Hyland, F., Trahar, S., Anderson, J. and Dickens, A., (2008). A Changing World: The Internationalisation Experiences of Staff and Students (Home and International) in UK Higher Education. Escalate and LLAS report.

Ibrahim, A.R., Nik Yusoff, N.M.R. and Kamarudin, M.Y., (2016). Mobile Learning Quality of Education and Increase in Student Discipline. *Creative Education.* 7(4). April 11.

International Council of Nurses, (2008). International Council of Nurses Asia Nursing Workforce Profile. Geneva, Switzerland.

International University, (2011). Proceedings of the 3rd International Conference of Teaching and Learning (ICTL 2011). Malaysia: INTI International University.

Ismail, N., (2006). The Impact of the Malaysia-United Kingdom B.Ed. Twinning Programme on the Teachers' Personal and Professional Development. Jabatan Bahasa Inggeris, Institut Perguruan Bahasa-Bahasa Antarabangsa.

Jantan, M., Chan, H., Shanon, S. and Sibly, S., (2005). Enhancing Quality of Faculty in Private Higher Education Institutions in Malaysia. Penang. National Higher Education Research Institute.

Jedin, M.H. and Saad, N. M., (2006). A Preliminary Study on Gender and Learning Style in Malaysian Higher Learning Institutions: Evidence From A Cultural Perspective. The Higher Education Research and Development Society of Australasia Conference.

Jeffreys, M., (2012). Nursing Student Retention: Understanding the Process and Making a Difference. Springer Publishing Company.

Jin, L. and Cortazzi, M. (2013a). Cultures of Learning: What can we learn from international students? Retrieved February, 27, 2017 from http://focusoninternationalstudents-eorg.eventbrite.com/# British Council.

Jin, L. and Cortazzi, M. (2013b). Introduction: Research and Levels of Intercultural Learning, In: Jin, L. and Cortazzi, M. (eds.) Researching intercultural learning: investigations in language and education. Basingstoke: Palgrave Macmillan. 1-17.

Jin, L. and Cortazzi, M. (2012). Researching intercultural learning. Investigations in language and education. Basingstoke: Palgrave Macmillan. 1-17.

Johnson, A., Hong, H., Groth, M, and Parker, S., (2011). Learning and development: promoting nurses ' performance and work attitudes. Journal of Advanced Nursing. 67(3). 609-20.

Joy, S. and Kolb, D.A. (2009). Are there cultural differences in learning style? International Journal of Intercultural Relations. 33. 69–85.

Juhary, J., (2007). Pedagogy Considerations for e-learning in a Military Learning Environment. MERLOT Journal of Online Learning and Teaching. 3(4).

Karstadt, L., (2011). Viable Knowledge: The Centrality of Practice. EdD. Thesis. University of Hertfordshire.

Kim, Y. Y. (1988). Communication and cross-cultural adaptation: an integrative theory. Philadelphia. Multilingual Matters.

Kim, Y. Y., (1992). Development of Intercultural Identity. Paper presented at the Annual Conference of the International Communication Association. Miami.

Kim, Y. Y. (2001). Becoming intercultural: An integrative theory of communication and cross-cultural adaptation. Thousand Oaks, CA. SAGE.

Kim, Y.Y. and Ruben, B.D., (1988). Intercultural Transformation: A Systems Theory. In Kim, Y.Y., and Gudykunst, W.B. (Eds.). International and intercultural communication: Theories in intercultural communication. 299-321. Newbury Park, CA. SAGE.

Kirby, J.R., Knapper, C.K., Evans, C.J., Carty, A.E. and Gadula, C., (2003). Approaches to Learning at Work and Workplace. Chapter 3. indd 60. Workplace Learning Approaches among Support Staff in Universiti Teknologi Malaysia climate. International Journal of Training and Development. 7(1). 31-52.

Kitzinger, J., (2006). Focus Groups, in Qualitative Research in Health Care. Third Edition (eds C. Pope and N. Mays). Oxford. Blackwell Publishing Ltd.

Knight, J., (2003). Updated Internationalization definition. International Higher Education. 33. 2-3.
Knight, J., (2004). Internationalisation Remodelled: Definitions, Approaches and Rationales. Journal of Studies in International Education. 8(1). 5-31.
Knight, J., (2008). Higher Education in turmoil: The changing world of internationalization. Rotterdam, Netherlands. Sense.
Knight, J., (2010a). Quality dilemmas with regional education hubs and cities. In S. Kaur, M. Sirat, and W. Tierney (Eds.), Quality assurance and university rankings in higher education in the Asia Pacific: Challenges for universities and nations. Penang, Malaysia. Universiti Sains Malaysia Press.
Knight, J., (2010b). Regional education hubs: Rhetoric or reality? International Higher Education. 59. 20-21.
Knight, J., (2011). Education hubs: a fad, a brand, an innovation? Journal of Studies in International Education. 15(3). 221-40.
Knight, J., and Morshidi, S., (2011). The complexities and challenges of education hubs: Focus on Malaysia. Journal of Higher Education.
Knox, L., (2000). The shock of the new: Students' perceptions of a collaborative degree. Innovations in Education and Training International, 37(2): 87-96.
Kramsch, C., (2017). The Challenge of Globalization in Foreign Language Education. The Center for Advanced Research on Language Acquisition (CARLA) Keynote Speaker: University of California–Berkeley.
Lasanowski, V., (2009). International student mobility: Status report. London, UK. The Observatory on Borderless Higher Education.
Latif, S., (2017) A Harakah Daily columnist has written that the Merdaka spirit died with the Merdeka generation and the ruling elites have since created a system which abuses democracy to enslave the people. The Malaysian Insight. July 28.
Leask, B., (2005.) Internationalisation of the Curriculum: Teaching and Learning. In Carroll, J., and Ryan, J., (Eds.). *Teaching International Students: Improving Learning for All.* 119-129. London. Routledge.
Leask, B. and Carroll, J., (2011). Moving beyond 'wishing and hoping': internationalisation and student experiences of inclusion and engagement. Higher Education Research and Development, 30 (5). 647-659.
Leininger, M., (2011). Leininger's reflection on her ongoing father protective care research. Online Journal of Cultural Competence in Nursing and Healthcare. 1(2). 1–13.
Levy, S., Osborn, M. and Plunkett, M. (2003). An Investigation of International Students' Academic and Social Transition Requirements. [Online] Retrieved June 28, 2017 from http://www.qut.edu.au/talss/fye/papers03/Refereed Papers/Fullpapers/
Lewin, R., (2010). The Handbook of Practice and Research in Study Abroad: Higher Education and the Quest for Global Citizenship. USA. Routledge.
Li, Y., (2012). *Cultural Foundations of Learning: East and West.* Cambridge. Cambridge University Press.

Lillibridge, J. and Fox, S.D., (2005). RN to BSN Education: What do RNs Think? Nurse Educator. 30(1). 12-16.

Ling, P., Mazzolini, M. and Giridharan, B., (2014). Towards Post-Colonial Management of Transnational Education. Australian Universities Review. 56(2). 47-55.

Llopis, G., (2014). Leadership is about enabling the full potential in others. Forbes. Blog.

Lynch, K., (2013). Australian Universities' preparation and support for fly-in fly-out academics, PhD thesis. Global, Urban and Social Studies, RMIT University.

Lynette, R., (1990). From Nightingale to Now: Nurse Education in Australia. Sydney. Churchill Livingston.

Maben, J., Latter, S. and Clark, J.M., (2006). The Theory-Practice Gap:Impact of Professional-Bureaucratic Work Conflict on Newly Qualified Nurses. Journal of Advanced Nursing. 55(4). 465-77.

Malaysian Nurses Association, (2010). Professional organization for Malaysian nurses. http://mna.org.my/default.asp.

Malaysian Nursing Board, (2007). Guidelines on Standards and Criteria for Approval/Accreditation of Nursing Programmes. Kuala Lumpur. MNB.

Malaysian Nursing Board, (2008). Guidelines for Continuous Professional Development Programme for Nurses / Midwives. Putrajaya. Nursing Division Ministry of Health Malaysia.

Malaysian Qualifications Agency (MQA), (2009). Rating System for Malaysian Higher Education Institutions. Retrieved April 2, 2017 from: http://www.mqa.gov.my/SETARA09/index.cfm.

Malaysian Qualifications Agency (2010). Data from Malaysian qualifications agency. Retrieved April 2, 2017 from http://www.mqa.gov.my/.

Mallia, G., (2013). The Social Classroom Integrating Social Network Use in Education. Advances in Educational Technologies and Instructional Design. USA. Information Science Reference.

Mandel, I. S., (2009). Understanding Differences between Holistic, Alternative, and Complementary Medicine. Journal of Alternative and Complementary Medicine. 10(2). 405-407.

Mantzoukas, S. and Jasper, M., (2008). Types of Nursing Knowledge used to Guide Care of Hospitalised Patients. Journal of Advanced Nursing. 62(3). 381-326.

Marginson, S., (2011). Higher Education and Public Good. Higher Education Quarterly. 65(4). 411–433.

McHugh, M.D., and Lake, T. E., (2010). Understanding Clinical Expertise: Nurse Education, Experience, and the Hospital Context. *Research Nurse Health*. 33(4). 276–287.

McIver, M. P. and Arunasalam, N. D., (2011). Malaysian nursing students' perspectives on the efficacy of trans-national Higher Education. In International University (Ed.), Proceedings of the 3rd International Conference of Teaching and Learning. Malaysia. INTI International.

Merleau-Ponty, M., (1962). The Phenomenology of Perception. London. Routledge and Kegan Paul.

Merton, R, (1972). Insiders and outsiders; a chapter in the sociology of knowledge, American Journal of Sociology. 78(July). 9-47.

Ministry of Higher Education Malaysia, (2007-2010).The National Higher Education Action Plan. Putrajaya. Kementerian Pengajian Tinggi Malaysia. August 2007.

Ministry of Higher Education Malaysia. (2010). Development of Nursing Education in Malaysia-towards the year 2020. Universiti Teknologi MARA Shah Alam. University Publication Centre (UPENA).

Ministry of Women, Family and Community Development, (2004). Malaysia report to the United Nations Committee on the Elimination of Discrimination against Women. Kuala Lumpur. Malaysia.

Miola, E. and Ramat, P., (2015). Language across Languages: New Perspectives on Translation. Newcastle upon Tyne. Cambridge ScholarsPublishing.

Mohamed, M., (1991). The Way Forward – Vision 2020, Kuala Lumpur, Retrieved June 4, 2017 from: http://www.spke.jpm.my/vision.htm.

Mohamad, R., Rashdan, A. and Rashid, M., (2006). Transnational Education:Our Expectations and our Challenges. Is anyone listening? From teachers' and students' perspectives. Paper presented at the Conference: International education, a matter of heart. Kuala Lumpur, Malaysia.

Mohamad, M., (2008). The Malay Dilemma. Singapore. Times Book International.

Mok, K.H., (2008). Singapore's Global Education Hub Ambitions: University Governance Change and Transnational Higher Education. International Journal of Educational Management. 22. 527-546.

Mok, K. H. and Yu, K. M., (2013). Internationalization of Higher Educationin East Asia: Trends of Student Mobility and Impact on Education Governance. Devon. Routledge Critical Studies in Asian Education.

Monaghan, T., (2015). A critical analysis of the literature and theoretical perspectives on theory–practice gap amongst newly qualified nurses within the United Kingdom. Nurse Education Today. 35(8). e1–e7. August.

Montgomery, C., (2016). Transnational partnerships in higher education in China: The diversity and complexity of elite strategic alliances. London Review of Education. 14(1). April.

Morshidi, S., (2006). Transnational Higher Education in Malaysia: Balancing Costs and Benefits through Regulations. RIHE International Publication Series 10. Hiroshima University. Japan.

Muir, D. and Laxton, J.C., (2012). Experts by experience: the views of service user educators providing feedback on medical students' work based assessments. Nurse Education Today. 32. 146-150.

Mustapha, S.M. and Nik Abdul Rahman, N.S., (2011). Classroom Participation Patterns: A Case Study of Malaysian Undergraduate Students. EDUCARE: International Journal for Educational Studies. 3(2). 145

Mylopoulos, M. and Regehr., G., (2011). Putting the expert together again. Medical Education. 45(9). 920-926.

Nieto, Sonia (2010). Language, Culture, and Teaching: Critical Perspectives. 2. New York. Routledge.

Nightingale, F., (1859). Notes on Nursing: What it is and What it is Not. London. Harrison.

Ng, L.C., Tuckett, A.G., Fox-Young, S.K. and Kain, V.J., (2014). Exploring registered nurses' attitudes towards postgraduate education in Australia: An overview of the literature. Journal of Nursing Education and Practice. 4(2).

Nursing and Midwifery Board of Australia, (1981). Health Practitioner Regulation National Law. State and territorial nursing regulation authorities. NMBA.

Nursing and Midwifery Council, (2004). Standards of proficiency for pre-registration nurse education. London. NMC.

Nursing and Midwifery Council, (2007). Good health and good character. Guidance for educational institutions. London. NMC.

Nursing and Midwifery Council, (2008). Review of pre-registration nurse education: Report of consultation findings. London. NMC.

Nursing and Midwifery Council, (2010). Standards for Pre-registration Nursing Education. London, NMC.

Nursing and Midwifery Council, (2011). Standards of support learning and assessment in practice. The Code. London. NMC.

Nursing and Midwifery Board of Australia, (2016). Health Practitioner Regulation National Law. State and territorial nursing regulation authorities. NMBA.

Oakley, A., (1981). Interviewing women, in: H. Roberts (Ed) Doing Feminist Research. London. Routledge and Kegan Paul.

Oberg, K., (1960). Culture Shock: Adjustment to New Culture Environments. Practical Anthropology. 7. 177-182.

Ohmori, F., (2004). Japan's Policy Changes to Recognise Transnational Higher Education: Adaptation of the National System to Globalisation? London. The Observatory on Borderless Higher Education.

Ohnuki-Tierney, E., (1984) Native Anthropologists, American Ethnologist. 11.584–6.

Olson, D.H., (1977). Insiders? and outsiders? views of relationships: research studies, In: G. Levinger and H. L. Rausch (Eds) Close relationships: perspectives on the meaning of intimacy. Amhurst. University of Massachusettes Press.

Olson, C. L. and Kroeger, K. R. (2001). Global competency and intercultural sensitivity. Journal of Studies in International Education. 5. 116-137.

Organisation for Economic Co-operation and Development (2010). Education at a Glance: OECD Indicators. OECD. www.oecd.org/edu/eag

Ota, H., McCann, R. M., and Honeycutt, J. (2012). Inter-Asian variability in intergenerational communication. Human Communication Research, 38, 172–198.

Parker, D. R., (1999). Teaching, learning, and working with international students: A case study. Education Resources Information Center Reprinted Document.

Pasteur, L., (1854). Inaugural Address as Newly Appointed Professor and Dean (September 1854) at the Opening of the New Faculté des Sciences at Lille (7

December 1854). In René Vallery-Radot. The Life of Pasteur. Translated by Mrs. Devonshire, R.L., (1919). 76.

Patton, M.Q., (2014). Qualitative research and evaluation methods, Integrating Theory and Practice. (4th edition). London, SAGE.

Pelletier, D., Donoghue, J. and Duffield, C., Adams, A. and Brown, D., (1998). Why Undertake Higher Degrees in Nursing? Journal of Nursing Education. 37(9). 422-2.

Perley, B., (2011). Defying Maliseet Language Death: Emergent Vitalities of Language, Culture, and Identity in Eastern Canada. Lincoln. University of Nebraska Press.

Phillips, T., Schostak, J. and Tyler, J., (2000). Practice and assessment in nursing and midwifery: Doing it for real. In: ENB (ed.) Researching Professional Education. London. English National Board for Nursing, Midwifery and Health Visiting.

Phinney, J., (2003). Ethnic Identity and Acculturation. In Chun, K., Organista, P. and Marin, G., (Eds.). Acculturation: Advances in Theory, Measurement and Applied Research. 63-81. Washington, DC. American Psychological Association.

Polit, D., Beck, C., (2010). *Essentials of Nursing Research: Appraising Evidence for Nursing Practice.* Philadelphia. Wolters Kluwer Health/Lippincott.

Pullen, R. L., (2011). Get on the road to professional development. Nursing Made Incredibly Easy! 9(1). 5.

Race, R., (2011). Multiculturalism and Education. London: Continuum.

Race, R., (2013). International and Domestic Perspectives on Master's Level Delivery. A Presentation for Global Higher Education, Students and Immigration Policy: Implications for the Higher Education. London. Society for Research into Higher Education.

Rafferty, A.M., Xyrichis, A., and Caldwell, C., (2015). Post-graduate education and career pathways in nursing: a policy brief Report to Lord Willis. UK. Independent Chair of the Shape of Caring Review.

Reed, A., (2012). Nursing in Partnership with Patients and Carers. United Kingdom. Learning Matters.

Richardson, L., (2000). Writing a Method of Inquiry. In Denzin, N.K., and Lincoln, Y.S., (2005). Handbook of Qualitative Research. California. SAGE.

Robertson, S., (2000). A Class Act: ChangingTeachers' Work. Globalisation and the Stage. New York. Falmer Press.

Rosa, W., Santos, S., (2016). Introduction of the Engaged Feedback Reflective Inventory during a Preceptor Training Program. Journal for Nurses in Professional Development. 32(4).

Rudmin, F.W., (2009). Catalogue of Acculturation Constructs: Description of 126 taxonomies. 1918-2003. Online Readings in Psychology and Culture. 8(1).

Ryan, J., and Hellmundt, S., (2003). Excellence through Diversity: Internationalisation of Curriculum and Pedagogy. Paper presented at 17th IDP International Education Conference.

Ryan, J., (2011). Teaching and learning for international students: towards a transcultural approach. Teachers and Teaching: Theory and Practice. 17 (6). 631-648.

Saha, L. J. and Dworkin, A. G., (2009). International Handbook of Research on Teachers and Teaching Editors. New York. Springer.

Salmon, N., (1989). The logic of what might have been. Philosophical Review. 98. 3–33.

Sampath, J. M., Bankwala, Y., and Sampath, K., (2006). Leadership Development through Transforming Beliefs - A Malaysian Case Study. Paper presented at the IFTDO Conference.

Samuelowicz, K., (1987). Learning Problems of Overseas Students: Two Sides of a Story. Higher Education Research and Development. 6(2). 121-133.

Sanner, S., (2002). The Experiences of International Nursing Students in a Bacclaureate Nursing Program. Journal of Professional Nursing. 18(4). 206-213.

Savicki, V., (2008). Developing Intercultural Competence and Transformation. Sterling. Stylus Publishing.

Savin Baden, M., (2004). Achieving reflexivity: moving researchers from analysis to interpretation in collaborative enquiry. Journal of Social Work Practice. 18 (3). 365-378.

Sayadi, Z. A., (2007). An Investigation into First Year Engineering Students' Oral Classroom Participation: A Case Study. Unpublished Master Thesis. Universiti Teknologi Malaysia.

Schober, M, M., (2013). Factors influencing the development of advanced practice nursing in Singapore. PhD thesis. Sheffield Hallam University, United Kingdom.

Schutz, A., (1964). Collected papers II: studies in social theory. Brodersen, A. (ed.). The Hague. Martinus Nijhoff.

Schutz, A., (1976). The Stranger. In 'Race and Ethnic Relations.' Bowker, G. and Carrier, J. (eds). London. Hutchison.

Schwab, J., (2004). The Practical: A Language for Curriculum. The Curriculum Studies Reader. In Flinders, D.J., and Thornton, S.J., (Eds.) NY. Routledge-Falmer.

Scott, J.C., (1996). Domination and the Arts of Resistance Hidden Transcripts. New Haven and London. Yale University Press.

Scully, N.J., (2011). The theory-practice gap and skill acquisition: an issue for nursing education. Collegian. 18(2). 93-8.

Seale, C., (2004). Researching Society and Culture. London. Routledge.

Selmer, J., and Lauring, J. (2010). Self-initiated academic expatriates: Inherent demographics and reasons to expatriate. European Management Review. 7(3). 169-179.

Selvarajah, C., and Meyer, D. (2008). One nation, three cultures: Exploring dimensions that relate to leadership in Malaysia. Leadership and Organization Development Journal. 29. 693–712.

Shagar, L.K., (2017). Unite in religious harmony. The Sun. Online. Sunday, 5 February.
Shakya, A. and Horsfall, J., (2000). ESL Undergraduate Nursing Students in Australia: Some Experiences. Nursing and Health Studies. 2(3). 163-171.
Shiffrin, R. M., and Schneider, W., (1977). Controlled and Automatic Human Information Processing: Perceptual Learning, Automatic Attending and a General Theory. Psychological Review. 84. 127-190.
Silverman, D., (2006). Interpreting Qualitative Data: Methods for Analysing Talk, Text and Interaction. London. SAGE.
Sirkeci, I. (2013). Transnational Marketing and Transnational Consumers. Heidelberg, New York: Springer.
Skeggs, B., (2002). Techniques for telling the reflexive self, in T. May (ed.). Qualitative Research in Action. London. SAGE. 349-374.
Shamsudin, N., (2006). Better Late than Never. Journal of Advanced Nursing. 30th Anniversary editorial. 53(3). 262-3.
Smith, L., (2009). Sinking in the sand? Academic work in an offshore campus of an Australian university. Higher Education Research and Development. 28(5). 467-479.
Smullen, A. and Phua, K, H., (2015). Comparing the Health Care Systems of High-Performing Asian Countries. Asia and Pacific Policy Studies. 2(2). 347–355.
Srinivasan, N., (2012). Care giver's reaction after covert action. Special theme. 54(3). 276-277.
Stein-Parbury, J., (2000). Nursing Around the World: Australia. Online Journal of Issues in Nursing. 5(2). 1-10.
Sturdy, A. and Gabriel, Y., (2000). Missionaries, Mercenaries or Car Salesmen? MBA Teaching in Malaysia. Journal of Management Studies. 37(7). 979-999.
Sumaco, F. T., Imrie, B. C., and Hussain, K. (2014). The Consequence of Malaysian National Culture Values on Hotel Branding. Procedia-Social and Behavioral Sciences. 144. 91-101.
Sundler, A J., Pettersson, A., Berglund, M., (2015). Undergraduate nursing students' experiences when examining nursing skills in clinical simulation laboratories with high-fidelity patient simulators: A phenomenological research study. Nurse Education Today. 35(12). 1257-61.
Tan, P.L. and Pillay, H., (2008). Understanding Learning Behaviour of Malaysian Adult Learners: A Cross-Cultural Sensitive Framework. Education Research Policy Practice. 7. 85-97.
Tani, M., (2005). Quiet, but only in class: Reviewing the in-class participation of Asian students [Electronic Version]. Retrieved May 22, 2012 from http://www.mendeley.com/research/quiet-only-class-reviewing-inclass-participation-asian-students/.
Taylor, C. and White, S., (2000). Practising Reflexivity in Health Care. Making knowledge. Buckingham. Open University press.
Temple, B. and Young, A., (2004). Qualitative Research and Translation Dilemmas. Online. August.

Teras, H.M., (2013). Dealing with "learning culture shock" in multicultural authentic e-learning. University Of Wollongong, Faculty of Social Sciences.

Thomas, E., (2005). Globalisation, cultural diversity and teacher education. In C. Cullingford and S. Gunn (Eds.) Globalisation, Education and Culture Shock.

Triandis, H. C., (1995). Individualism and Collectivism: New Directions in Social Psychology. Boulder. Westview Press.

Trice, H.M., and Beyer, J.M., (1993). *The Cultures of Work Organisations*. Englewood Cliffs, NJ. Prentice Hall.

Tuohy, D., (1999). The Inner World of Teaching: Exploring Assumptions Which Promote Change and Development. London. Falmer Press.

Turner, C., and Trompenaars, F., (1993). The Seven Cultures of Capitalism. London. Piatkus.

United Kingdom Council for International Student Affairs, (2008). International students and culture shock. UK, UKCISA. December.

United Kingdom Central Council for Nursing, Midwifery and Health Visiting. (1986). Project 2000. A New Preparation for Practice. London. UKCC.

United Kingdom Central Council for Nursing, Midwifery and Health Visiting. (2001). Requirements for Pre-Registration Nursing Programmes. London. UKCC.

UNESCO / Council of Europe, (2002). Code of Good Practice in the Provision of Transnational Education. Bucharest: UNESCO/CEPES.

UNESCO / OECD, (2005). Guidelines for Quality Provision in Cross-border Higher Education. UNESCO and OECD. Paris.

Van Manen, M. (2014). Phenomenology of practice: Meaning-giving methods in phenomenological research and writing. California. Left Coast Press.

Van Bogaert, P., Timmermans, O., Weeks, S. M. and Van Heusden, D., Wouters, K., and Franck, E. (2014). Nursing unit teams matter: Impact of unit-level nurse practice environment, nurse work characteristics, and burnout on nurse reported job outcomes, and quality of care, and patient adverse events. A cross-sectional survey. International Journal of Nursing Studies. 51(8).

Volet, S.E., and Jones, C., (2012). Cultural Transitions in Higher Education: Individual Adaptation, Transformation and Engagement. To appear in S. Karabenick and T. Urdan (Eds). *Advances in Motivation and Achievement:Transitions Across Schools and Cultures*. Bingley, UK. Emerald. 17.

Varutharaju, E., and Ratnavadivel, N., (2014). Enhancing Higher Order Thinking Skills through Clinical Simulation Malaysian Journal of Learning and Instruction. 11. 75-100.

Walker, G., (2010). East is East and West is West. Maidenhead. SRHE and Open University Press.

Wang, V,V,X., (2010) Higher Education Leadership. International Journal of Adult Vocational. 1(2). i-iii.

Wan Husin, W. N. (2011). Budi-Islam; Its roles in the construction of Malay identity in Malaysia. International Journal of Humanities and Social Science. 1. 132–142.

Wan Yusoff, W. F., (2011). Does organizational culture influence firm performance in Malaysia? International Journal of Multidisciplinary Research. 1(3). July.

Watkins, D, S., and Ryan, J, L., (2015). Reasons for application and expectations from a post-registration degree: Views of Omani nurses and their managers. Journal of Nursing Education and Practice. 5(4).

Weber, M., (1947). The Theory of Social and Economic Organisation. Translated by Henderson, A.M. and Talcott Parsons. The Free Press and Falcon's Bring Press.

Welikala, T. (2013) 'Inter-Perspective Pedagogy: Rethinking Culture and Learning in Multicultural Higher Education in the United Kingdom', in Jin, L. and Cortazzi, M. (eds.) Researching intercultural learning. Investigations in language and education. Basingstoke: Palgrave Macmillan. 36-57.

Wenger E (1998). Communities of Practice: Learning, meaning and identity. Cambridge, Cambridge University Press.

Wenger, E., (2000). Communities of practice and social learning systems. Organization. 7(2). 225-246.

Whyte, D.A., Lugton, J., Fawcett, T.N., (2000). Fit for Purpose: The Relevance of Masters Preparation for the Professional Practice of Nursing. A 10-year follow-up Study of Post graduate Nursing Courses in the University of Edinburgh. Journal Advanced Nursing. 31(5). 1072–80.

Widdowson, H.G., (1990). Aspects of Language Teaching. Oxford. OUP.

Wilton, L., and Constantine, M., (2003). Length of Residence, Cultural Adjustment Difficulties, and Psychological Distress Symptoms in Asian and Latin American International College Students. Journal of College Counseling. 6(2). 177–186.

Wolcott, H. (1999) Ethnography: A Way of Seeing, Altamira Press, Walnut Creek. Education Research International.

Wright, H., Singh, M., and Race, R., (2012). Precarious International Multicultural Education. Hegemony, Dissent and Rising Alternatives. Netherlands. Sense Publishers.

Wu, H.S., Garza, E. and Guzman, N., (2015). International Student's Challenge and Adjustment to College. Education Research International.

Yaakup. H, Eng, T. C. and Shah, S. A., (2014). *Does Clinical Experience Help Oncology Nursing Staff to Deal with Patient Pain Better than Nurses from other Disciplines?* Knowledge and Attitudes Survey Amongst Nurses in a Tertiary Care in Malaysia. Asian Pacific Journal of Cancer Prevention. 15. 4885–4891.

Yamat, H., Mustapa Umar, N.F. and Mahmood, M.I., (2014). Upholding the Malay Language and Strengthening the English Language Policy: An Education Reform. International Education Studies. 7(13).

Zawawi D., 2008, Cultural Dimensions among Malaysian Employees, Int. Journal of Economics and Management 2(2). 409 – 426.

Ziguras, C., (2007). Towards an Internationalised Higher Education Policy. Presentation to the Australian International Education Conference. Melbourne, 10 October 2007.

Ziguras, C. and McBurnie, G., (2015). Governing Cross-Border Higher Education. London: Routledge.

Ziguras, C., (2016). And Fairness for All? Equity and the international student cohort. Student Equity in Australian Higher Education. 207-220.

Index

academic achievement ... 89, 90, 103
Acquisition of knowledge 45
Asian students 35, 43
Australia...................................... 103
Australian Health Professionals Regulation Agency AHPRA 9
Australian Vice-Chancellors' Committee 109
Bahasa................. 57, 68, 73, 75, 120
Biggs............... 5, 27, 47, 49, 80, 110
Code of Good Practice in the Provision of Transnational Education 4
commercialisation 14, 46
Continuous Professional Education 4, 22, 24
Epistemological reflexivity 55
epitome of good thinking............. 35
flying faculty 5, 80, 81, 83, 102, 104, 108, 113, 115, 118, 125
global movements 31
Goffman................................. 68, 73
Hammersley................................ 72
hermeneutic phenomenology 65
hierarchical society 34
hierarchical teaching method 34
Hofstede .. 31, 34, 35, 36, 38, 39, 76, 81, 83, 115
Individualism-collectivism 37
interculturalism............................ 34
International Council of Nurses ICN.. 8, 39
international students 121
lifelong learning 3, 12, 21, 23, 94

Long-term versus short term orientation 39
Malaysian Ministry of Health 118
Malaysian Nursing Board .. 1, 4, 9, 20
Malaysian Qualifications Agency MQA 10
Masculinity-femininity 38
memorisation 34, 85, 87
Merton................................. 65, 71
multi-ethnic 37, 47, 55
nurse-led 98, 111
Offshore teaching 47
overseas students 49
Power distance 34
quality assurance .. 14, 15, 47, 49, 51
Schutz 55, 67, 71
Sirkeci.. 3
Skeggs 53, 54, 66, 120
the UK 103, 107, 109, 110
TNHE classroom 32, 39, 80, 120
TNHE experiences 101
TNHE programmes ... 68, 94, 98, 102, 103, 108, 109, 110, 112, 118, 119, 120, 122, 123, 125
top-up degree 4, 7, 9, 10, 23, 24, 25, 29, 41, 48, 76, 125
Transnational space 3
Tun Dr Mahathir Mohamed 4
Uncertainty avoidance 36
UNESCO 4, 13, 14, 50
upbringing.................................... 45
Van Bogaert 77
WHO 6, 55, 96, 105
willingness to conform................. 31
World Health Organisation 115

www.ingramcontent.com/pod-product-compliance
Lightning Source LLC
Chambersburg PA
CBHW061452300426
44114CB00014B/1941